CONTENTS

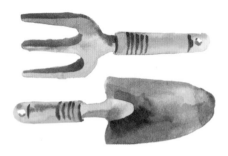

Introduction

||||||||||||||||||||||||||||||||||||||

Our culture is one that evolved from a lifestyle of thrift and reuse from the pioneer days and the years of the world wars to one of convenience and consumerism in the post-war years, and the result has been a lot of waste—cans, bottles, plastic bags, and so forth. But for several years now, the pendulum has been swinging back toward more conscientiousness. The political and social movement toward "zero-waste" living is now decidedly with us, as seen in magazine articles, books, and political debate—not to mention the people quietly living it. These days, some people are so extremely efficient at this that they produce less than one bag of trash per year.

That's not necessarily realistic for most of us.

But it *is* realistic for most of us to look at our daily lives and see where we can recycle, reuse . . . and also regrow—the main subject of this book.

Once you get started, living a low-waste or no-waste lifestyle can become almost like a game, but a game with tangible results. More and more, consumers young and old are entering into a no-waste lifestyle for a variety of reasons and out of a variety of personal perspectives. Some people arrive here out of a "green" attitude and a need to protect the planet, while for others it is an intense need for self-sufficiency and a wish to be prepared for any eventuality.

Whatever the motivation, those wishing to practice a no-waste lifestyle have many practical ways to get started.

THE NO-WASTE LIFESTYLE

No-waste consumers are always looking for ways to cut down on trash, save water, and green up their home and garden. There are multiple ways to do this. First,

Re   lore

KATIE ELZER-PETERS

COOL
SPRINGS
PRESS

For my husband, Joe, my CWO (Chief Watering Officer)
and plant–zoo wrangler when I'm traveling.

Inspiring | Educating | Creating | Entertaining

Brimming with creative inspiration, how-to projects, and useful information to enrich your everyday life, Quarto Knows is a favorite destination for those pursuing their interests and passions. Visit our site and dig deeper with our books into your area of interest: Quarto Creates, Quarto Cooks, Quarto Homes, Quarto Lives, Quarto Drives, Quarto Explores, Quarto Gifts, or Quarto Kids.

10 9 8 7 6 5 4 3 2 1

ISBN: 978-0-7603-6160-3

Library of Congress Cataloging-in-Publication Data

Names: Elzer-Peters, Katie, author.
Title: No-waste kitchen gardening : regrow your leftover greens, pits, seeds, and more / by Katie Elzer-Peters.
Description: Minneapolis, Minnesota : Cool Springs Press, 2018. | Includes index.
Identifiers: LCCN 2018026106 | ISBN 9780760361603 (pb)
Subjects: LCSH: Food crops. | Kitchen gardens.
Classification: LCC SB175 .E55 2018 | DDC 635--dc23
LC record available at https://lccn.loc.gov/2018026106

Editor: Madeleine Vasaly / Alyssa Lochner
Project Manager: Jordan Wiklund
Art Director: James Kegley
Cover Designer: Emily Weigel
Layout: Laura Shaw Design
Photography: Kirsten Boehmer, except where otherwise noted

Printed in China

MIX
Paper from
responsible sources
FSC® C008047

when you're shopping, look for items in containers that can be recycled or reused. When possible, buy in bulk and buy produce that isn't wrapped at all. Keep yard waste (leaves, twigs, weeds, grass clippings) out of the landfill by creating your own compost pile or check into potential municipal compost programs.

A little ingenuity will reveal lots of small ways to conserve and reuse water that will add up to big environmental savings. Install rain barrels at your downspouts and use them to water your container gardens and raised beds. Keep a 5-gallon bucket handy in each shower to collect runoff while you're waiting for the water to heat up. You can use that to water houseplants. Let water you use to boil pasta and vegetables cool down after cooking, then use it to water plants outside.

We often think about gardening as being a "green" activity, but gardening can actually generate a lot of waste: new plants in plastic containers, commercial mulch, and fertilizers are

It's possible to regrow lots of your kitchen scraps, such as carrots, onions, and lettuce. You'll save time and money, and have a little fun too!

all sources of waste. The first place to start with no-waste gardening is to reuse all of the biomass (yard clippings) produced in your yard. From twigs to weeds to clippings to last season's annuals, your yard produces a lot of organic material. Instead of sending it away, chip it up to use as mulch, or build a compost pile and use it to improve your soil.

Instead of buying new plants in plastic containers every year, learn how to grow your own from seed. Participate in plant exchanges where everyone brings plants to swap with one another. Old pots, yogurt cups, and Tupperware containers with missing lids are all viable options for plant sharing. Before you throw anything away, think about how you might be able to reuse it. Filing cabinets, old wheelbarrows, and old furniture make fun and funky container gardens. Old tools can be used to make interesting trellises or stakes.

Finally, no-waste living means cooking what you need and eating what you cook, but it also means squeezing every last bit of life out of your ingredient list. If you pay attention when you cook with fruits and vegetables, you'll see that you end up with a sizable pile of produce that would normally end up in the compost heap.

Not so fast! We're now approaching the ultimate form of no-waste living. You can actually regrow a lot of those kitchen scraps rather than composting them. Talk about taking no-waste living to the extreme!

NO—WASTE KITCHEN GARDENING

This is what you're here for—a lifestyle in which even the scrap food material you might compost can be reused in some way. After you read this book, you will never look at a grocery store, farmers' market, or recipe the same way again. Each time you pick up a fruit or vegetable, your first thought will be, "I wonder if I can regrow this?"

When we cook, we frequently discard plant parts that we might—just might—put to further purpose. You can throw the scraps leftover from making a soup or a salad in the compost pile, but you might also be able to use many of those scraps to regrow almost a whole garden, right from your kitchen counter or a small piece of your yard.

And there are lots of reasons to do just that.

Why Regrow Kitchen Scraps?

Save money. Will regrowing everything really reduce your grocery bill? It depends on what you eat and how dedicated you are to regrowing. Some head lettuce, for example, can be regrown. If it costs $4 a head at the grocery store and you can regrow at least one additional whole head of leaves, that's $4 you didn't have in your pocket before.

Fresh herbs add so much flavor to meals, but they are also pricey. Thankfully, they're also pretty easy to grow from the bits and pieces you buy at the farmers' market.

Keep fresh ingredients on hand. With a well-stocked pantry, you can easily whip up something tasty for dinner without going to market. However, the finishing touches (herbs and greens, mostly) taste much better when fresh. You don't have to settle for dried when you have a nice row of little cuttings growing on your windowsill.

Reduce kitchen waste. We hope that you're already composting. If you're not, you can learn a little bit about that in Chapter 1. It's easy and will cut down on your garbage bill. Plus, it gives you a great nutritious soil amendment and mulch for your outdoor garden. People who regrow what they can and compost the rest are flushing almost no waste down a garbage disposal and are sending minimal amounts of refuse to the landfill.

Control your food source. Recent years have seen a rise in food-borne illnesses, such as *E. coli* infections, from foods previously thought to be perfectly safe, such as lettuce. This is usually traced to fertilizers spread over commercial food production fields and handling of produce during harvest. Such risks disappear entirely when you are regrowing your own edibles on your countertop or in your own garden, where you can control exactly what goes on them.

Save money on garden plants. Some kitchen leftovers you root can then be planted out in the garden to grow into full-fledged, harvestable plants. The more plants you root from leftovers, the fewer transplants you will have to buy for spring planting.

Have fun! It is a flat-out rewarding and entertaining experience to take plant material that was destined for the compost heap, garbage disposal, or trash bin and turn it instead into a productive, growing plant on your countertop or in your garden. I especially like watching carrot tops grow—they're pretty as well as tasty.

GET KIDS INVOLVED

All of the projects in this book are great for kids because they're relatively simple and almost guaranteed to produce interesting results. Kids get the chance to learn about where their food comes from while taking in bit of botany and horticulture at the same time. When kids need a science project, anything with plants is always a hit.

HOW TO USE THIS BOOK

No-Waste Kitchen Gardening opens with a chapter on the basic science and practice of regrowing kitchen scraps. Here, you'll learn to understand plant parts, the growing cycle of edible herbs, vegetables, and fruits, and how to make use of this cycle when regrowing kitchen leftovers. Then you'll get to the good stuff: a series of chapters detailing how to regrow edibles according to different forms of propagation—from rooting vegetables in water to collecting seeds and planting them to produce your own seedlings for garden transplant. Your kitchen will never be the same.

No-waste kitchen gardening is calling you. Let's get started, shall we?

No-Waste Kitchen Gardening: How It Works and How to Do It

Plants are pretty incredible living things. The tiniest of seeds contains everything needed to grow tall oak trees and long squash vines. You can cut pieces off of some plants, stick the pieces in water, and watch them grow roots. Some plants grow, flower, produce seeds, and then die back, only to emerge again the following year from their roots. Some of these perennial plants may last for many decades; other short-lived annuals live their lives in a flash, barely lasting a single growing season before fading and wilting.

To regrow kitchen scraps, you'll need to get a handle on some basic plant science (botany). Depending on the vegetable, it may be the seeds, the roots, the leaves, the stems, or some modified version of stems that you are eating, so you'll need to be able to identify which part you're trying to regrow and where that plant part fits in the plant life cycle. That information will help you know what to expect from your regrowing efforts.

There are many plants that are possible to regrow that aren't covered in this book. I'm focusing on those that are easier and more productive, because the goal here is not only to eat well, but to have fun doing it. But with the information in this chapter, you'll have a foundation for regrowing plants I don't cover as well as those I do.

PARTS OF THE PLANT: ROOT YOUR SHOOTS AND EAT YOUR LEAVES

As you learn about the finer points of no-waste kitchen gardening, there's one overarching principle to keep in mind: **any plant part you want to regrow must have some type of stem-growing tip in it or on it.**

What is called the "growing tip" can take different forms across different types of plants and different parts of plants. Roots have growing tips and so do stems. You'll hear more about this in the individual plant-part descriptions. When you're looking at a plant part and trying to determine whether you can regrow it at all, the key is to find a point that can expand into more stems, more branches, more leaves, and/or eventually, flowers.

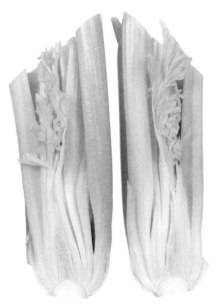

The growing tip in a bunch of celery is actually buried deep within the stalks that we eat.

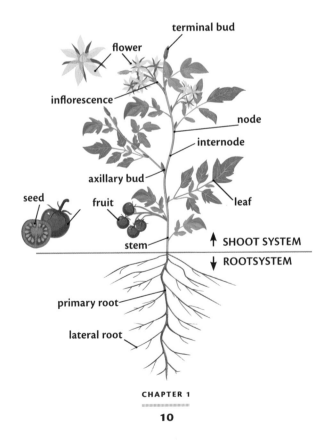

Roots

Roots are the underground parts of the plant from which the plant takes up food and water. Roots have growing tips at their ends so that the roots will keep growing down into the soil, but they do not have stem-growing tips anywhere along the roots. If you want to regrow these vegetables you have to look for root vegetables with the tops intact or, if there are no leaves, at least plant parts where the tops have been not sliced off.

Root vegetables include:

- Beets
- Carrots
- Parsnips
- Radishes
- Rutabagas
- Sweet potatoes
- Turnips
- Yams

Some of our favorite vegetables for regrowing are roots: beets, carrots, turnips, parsnips, and radishes. You won't get full new carrots to eat, but you'll get some delicious greens.

One sweet potato plant produces multiple tuberous roots.

There are two main types of roots that we eat: *taproots* and *tuberous roots*. Most of the root vegetables we eat fall into the taproot category, including carrots, turnips, and radishes. If the top of the taproot where the leaves sprout is still intact, you can regrow some leaves to enjoy, but you cannot regrow the taproot itself.

Sweet potatoes and cassava are plants that have tuberous roots. The difference between these plants and those with taproots is that you can grow a whole new plant from a piece of the tuberous root. This is not a difficult process but it does involve many steps (see Chapter 2).

Stems

Stems are usually aboveground, but there are modified stems that grow below-ground or half aboveground and half belowground. What distinguishes a stem from a root is that it has a growing tip and buds that can sprout new branches that will eventually form flowers (and then fruits and seeds). The stem is the structure that supports the leaves, flowers, seeds, fruits, and other aboveground plant parts. Collectively, all of these parts are called the *shoot*.

A tree trunk is essentially a big stem with branches and leaves. How does that relate to what you're eating? If there are branches or leaves coming out of the plant part that you're eating, that's the stem. If there are little buds on what you're eating, that's a stem. The stem also has a growing tip at the top where new growth emerges. If there are no buds where a new plant could form, then it isn't a whole stem.

Stems are the most complicated plant parts that we eat because they come in many different forms and there are many sub-parts.

Stem vegetables that look like stems include:

- Bunching onions (green onions or scallions)

- Kohlrabi

- Leeks

Leeks are plant stems.

Stem vegetables/fruits that look mostly like stems if you buy the whole plant include:

- Celery (the stem is in the center of a celery bunch)

- Lettuce (if you buy a complete head of lettuce)

- Pineapple (the top)

Underground Modified Stem Vegetables.
To complicate things, some stems grow primarily underground. How do you distinguish them from roots? Underground stems have buds (or eyes) that can sprout new stems and leaves. Here are some variations of underground stems:

- **Tubers** are fleshy modified stems. Potatoes are an example of tubers. The "eyes" of potatoes are actually little branch buds.

- **Rhizomes** are modified stems that grow horizontally underground and have buds on them. They might be somewhat fleshy, but they are not as fleshy as a potato. Ginger is a rhizome.

- **Bulbs** are another form of modified stem that grows underground. The growing tip is actually buried far inside the bulb, protected by modified leaves, called *bulb scales*. Onions are bulbs, but the portion you eat is actually a modified leaf.

Leaves

Leaves have two parts: the leaf blade (what you think of as a leaf) and the petiole, or leaf stem, which connects the leaf blade to the plant stem.

There are two types of leaves: simple and compound. Simple leaves are composed of one leaf blade and one petiole. Where the petiole attaches to the plant stem there is usually a bud. That section of the plant is called a *node*. Compound leaves are composed of several leaflets attached to a petiole that attaches to the plant stem. Tomato leaves are compound leaves.

Most leaf vegetables and herbs are easy to identify because they *look* like tree leaves but are edible. Some of these leaf vegetables and herbs are sold as intact plants (lettuce and cabbage come to mind). Others are sold on intact stems (fresh herbs, such as basil, cilantro, and rosemary). In order to easily regrow leaf vegetables, some of the plant stem needs to be attached.

Common Leaf Vegetables

- Basil
- Cabbage (usually sold as a head or stem)

- Cilantro
- Collards
- Dill

Leaves, such as dill, lettuce, and flat-leaf parsley seen here, are some of the most nutrient-dense vegetable parts we can eat.

- Endive

- Kale (usually sold as bunches of leaves bound together)

- Lettuce (Loose leaf lettuce cannot be rerooted. Head lettuce can, if the bottom of the stem is still intact.)

- Swiss chard (Single stalks are leaves with no stems.)

- Parsley

- Rosemary

- Spinach

- Thyme

Common Leaf Stem Vegetables

A couple of popular vegetables, celery and rhubarb, are actually leaf stems (petioles)—the "stalks" that you eat are the leaf stems. Celery that is sold as a whole plant with the bottom intact can be rerooted. Rhubarb is usually sold as cut up stalks that can't be rerooted.

Remember: no growing tip or bud means that no regrowing is possible.

Artichokes are flowers that we eat before they open up.

This broccoli is ready for picking. Once broccoli flowers, it is too late to harvest.

Flowers

People are often surprised to recognize how often they are eating flowers. But some of your favorite edibles are flowers, flower heads (one big plant part filled with a bunch of tiny flowers), or flowers on stalks.

Flowers are the reproductive parts of the plant. They represent the "in-between" state between the stems and leaves and the seeds. Stems have growing tips that can keep growing, while seeds have everything needed to grow a new plant. Flowers have neither, and their little cells are hardwired neither to reroot nor to regrow. They are hardwired to produce seeds.

Once a plant has transitioned into flower mode, it is difficult to keep it from flowering. For most of our edibles, flowering means either letting the plant continue until it produces a seed we can replant, or throwing the plant part in the compost and starting over.

That's one reason why, if you're going to take stem cuttings to root (from herbs, for example), you need to take the cuttings before the plant starts to flower. If you take cuttings from a flowering basil plant, for example, you're going to have a hard time getting delicious leaves to grow, since the plant is now programmed to flower. Or, if you stick a broccoli stem in fresh water after cutting off the bottom, the little green bits at the top will open up into flowers, but little else will happen.

Flowers We Eat

- Artichoke
- Broccoli
- Cauliflower

Fruits and Seeds

Many of the "vegetables" we eat are actually fruits. From a technical botanical sense, anything that has seeds within the structure is a fruit. (The seeds can also be *on* the fruit; strawberries wear their seeds on the outside of the fruit.)

Here are some common fruits and seeds that we eat:

- Avocados
- Bananas
- Beans (dry)
- Beans (fresh, like green beans)
- Blackberries
- Cantaloupe
- Chickpeas
- Corn
- Cucumbers
- Eggplant
- Mung beans
- Oranges
- Peanuts
- Peas
- Peppers
- Popcorn
- Raspberries
- Tomatoes
- Watermelons
- Zucchinis

Avocados are fruits.

Marino Branch
Brainse Marino
Tel: 8336297

It's worth experimenting with the seeds inside fruit, because they offer another way to regrow plants. You can't cut an apple in half and root it, but you can take the seeds out of the apple, prepare a seed, and plant it. Seeds that are dry and can be removed from the fruit can be planted directly—dried corn, dried peas, and peanuts are good candidates for this. Squishy seeds are not fully developed and won't grow: zucchini, for example, does not contain dried seeds because you eat it before it gets to that point. Bananas are the same. Watermelon seeds, though, can be planted.

The bottom line is: when in doubt, experiment! That's the whole point of this book. You may well be surprised to find that you can regrow a piece of that unusual fruit or vegetable you purchased at the grocery store. But to do that you need to know a bit about how plants grow.

HOW PLANTS GROW

Most of the plants we eat come from flowering plants, which all have a similar basic life cycle, with a few variations between types.

The Plant Life Cycle

1. A seed lands on the soil or is planted.

2. The seed sprouts (germinates) and grows, producing leaves.

3. Eventually, the plant produces flowers. Plants that are producing flowers are in the reproductive stage—everything is geared toward producing seeds.

4. The flowers open and are pollinated by insects, other animals, or wind.

5. The base of the flower (the ovary) swells into a fruit and seeds are produced within the fruit.

6. The seeds mature and are dispersed. The plant life cycle starts over.

REGROWING PLANTS

"What you see is not always what you get" is a major theme in no-waste kitchen gardening.

When you buy a young transplant or packet of seeds from the garden center, you're buying something that is ready to go in the ground or in a pot immediately.

The ovary of the flower is what swells to become fruit. You can see a zucchini fruit developing at the bottom of the zucchini flower.

You are essentially planting at an early stage of the plant's cycle and simply finishing it off.

The process looks a little different when you are regrowing food from leftover vegetables that were purchased originally to eat rather than to plant. Your goal is not necessarily to grow a finished plant, but rather to shrewdly take advantage of the plant's life-cycle stage. For example, no-waste carrot use isn't about growing new carrots, but about growing the leaf portion to use as greens. The carrots you've purchased in a bundle from the grocery store have already passed the point in their cycle where you can grow new roots. The no-waste gardener is now making use of a different stage in the life cycle.

TYPES OF PLANT PROPAGATION

There are several ways in which to obtain new plants from old ones. In nature, plants propagate by

- spreading the seeds they've produced through the production of flowers and fruit, or

- spreading their roots, or

- extending other plant parts, which then take root and grow into new plants.

This last means is known as vegetative propagation, and it is a key technique for botanists and no-waste kitchen gardeners.

Buy beets with the tops intact, and you can regrow plenty of greens to enjoy on salads or for sautéing.

The top of one plant is grafted to the bottom of another plant to produce many of the fruits we enjoy eating. A piece of a known variety of fruit tree (such as a Honeycrisp apple) is snipped and allowed to grow together with a disease-resistant rootstock (a different variety of apple).

Vegetative Propagation: Regrowing Whole Plants and Plant Parts

There are some plant parts that you can just stick in water or soil, and they will reroot themselves. This is *vegetative propagation*. The specifics of how to do this are outlined in detail in many of the plant profiles throughout the rest of this book. When you regrow plants vegetatively rather than from seed, there are three possible results:

- An entire new plant will grow into a full new harvest. Potatoes are the best example of this, but onions, ginger root, and celery are also examples.

- The same plant will continue to grow. For example, you can place a head of lettuce in water (provided the bottom of the head is intact) and allow it to keep growing. You'll get more lettuce leaves to eat.

- Something completely different will grow. This mostly happens when you regrow root vegetable tops from such plants as carrots, turnips, radishes, or beets. You buy these vegetables primarily to eat the roots, but you can regrow the tops of the plants and enjoy greens until the plant runs out of gas.

Many edible plants that we eat come from vegetatively propagated stock. In plain language, this means a piece of a plant (called a *cutting*) was taken and rooted (planted) or grafted (allowed to grow together onto another supporting plant). Many popular fruits, especially apples, are grown in this way. So, if you eat a Granny Smith apple and plant the seeds, you're unlikely to end up with a Granny Smith apple. Citrus trees are almost all grown in this way. You can plant seeds from an orange, but there's no telling what kind of fruit you'll end up with. (Citrus plants are all incredibly complicated crosses between different species, and many are then vegetatively propagated. The citrus family tree is pretty interesting!)

TOOLS, MATERIALS, AND SUPPLIES

Now that you know the science behind no-waste kitchen gardening, you can start gathering the supplies you'll need to regrow some of your favorite fruits and vegetables.

In the spirit of no-waste gardening, challenge yourself to recycle and reuse containers, fit plants in a small amount of space outdoors, and, when you're successful saving seeds and multiplying your plants, share the bounty with friends and neighbors.

Because *No-Waste Kitchen Gardening* is not a comprehensive gardening book, in this chapter I've included the most important aspects of gardening that pertain to regrowing. I focus on how to squeeze a bit more out of materials you're already using to cook. If you want detailed instructions for long-term gardening, indoors or out, including tools and techniques that will take you through the four seasons, there are plenty of other books available. (I've included some of my favorites in the Resources section on page 124.)

Regrowing vegetables and fruits is almost more of a science experiment than anything else. Like a scientist, you'll want to keep a few simple supplies on hand so that you're always ready to regrow.

Containers

For regrowing plants in water, gather a mix of shallow trays, cups, small bowls, canning jars of various sizes, and a wide-mouthed vase or two.

To regrow small plants in soil, collect pots and containers with drainage holes. You'll want pots between 4 inches in diameter and 24 inches in diameter, depending on what you're regrowing. It's helpful to have trays for catching water and clear trays or domes for covering the containers. If you're sprouting many seeds at once, it's useful to have a seedling flat and a tray that fits under it to catch water.

I am almost always using old plastic takeout containers or cottage cheese containers with lids to sprout something—beans, spices, or other seeds.

Potting Soil

I generally recommend sterile soilless mix for most regrowing projects. This should not contain bacteria or fungi, which can cause plants you're regrowing to rot.

Tools

Regrowing requires just a few tools, but if you don't have these on hand, you'll be scrambling. Make sure to have a sharp knife for cutting off ends and tops, a pair of pruners or scissors to trim what you're growing, a watering can, a spray bottle for misting, and a fine mesh sieve for cleaning seeds. Planning to regrow plants with pits or nuts? Add a nutcracker to your list.

If you're growing plants outdoors, keep a soil knife or hand hoe around for planting and a four-tine cultivator for loosening the soil. While you can water outdoors with a watering can, a hose and watering wand will make quicker work of large areas.

Miscellaneous Supplies

There are just a few other supplies that you'll use up regularly and have to replenish. Buy a box of toothpicks (quality, strong toothpicks, not flimsy ones) to use to suspend bits of vegetables and seeds in water. Keep a roll of paper towels and a roll of plastic wrap nearby. Those are both used to keep moisture around a plant part while it is sprouting. I recommend disinfecting pruners, knives, and containers with Lysol® or isopropyl alcohol before cutting, trimming, or planting parts to regrow.

Any other supplies will be listed with the individual plant regrowing instructions.

WAYS TO REGROW

The following chapters are organized by the part of the plant you're regrowing and the associated growing technique you'll use. If you have a specific plant you'd like to regrow, consult the index—but be aware that there might be more than one way to do it! To give you a taste of what's coming, here's a brief description of what to expect.

Regrow Roots and Underground Stems in Soil

When you regrow roots and underground stems in the soil, you'll cut off a section of the plant, plant it in the soil, water it, and watch it grow. It's pretty simple! The results of growing these plant parts vary by plant, but it's fun and easy to do.

Regrow Stems and Modified Stems in Soil

Regrowing stems and modified stems in soil is much like regrowing roots and underground stems, except you'll usually have part of the roots attached to the top (stem) parts that you're regrowing. Again, results vary.

Regrow Stems and Whole Plants in Water

Regrowing stems and whole plants in water can be as simple as sticking your stem or cutting in a glass of water. The nuances are in understanding what to do with the results of your regrowing and how to prolong the harvest, usually by moving the plant parts into soil to continue developing.

HOW TO DO A GERMINATION TEST OR PRESPROUT SEEDS

Before you plant a bunch of seeds in the garden, do a germination test with a small number of seeds to see if they'll sprout.

Supplies:
You will need seeds, paper towels, and a plastic container with a lid
(or a plastic zipper bag).

1. Wet three paper towels.

2. Layer the towels one on top of the other and place them in the bottom
   of the plastic container with half the width of the towels hanging out.

3. Place three of each of the types of seeds you want to test on the wet
   paper towels.

4. Fold the other half of the paper towels over the seeds.

5. Put the lid on the container.

6. Place the container somewhere warm and dark for 4 to 6 days. (A kitchen
   cabinet works well for this.)

7. Check which seeds have started sprouting. Those are the ones you
   want to plant outside!

Growing Seeds

You might not think of seeds when you think of "regrowing," but growing seeds does fit into the no-waste kitchen garden mentality. Often you can save a few seeds from something you're cooking—for instance, winter squash. You can sometimes sprout some seeds from the spice cabinet or experiment with a few kernels of popcorn. You'll plant all of the seeds you're regrowing in soil, except for the avocado: you'll start that in water. It is often helpful to do a germination test on a few seeds before you attempt to sprout them all (see sidebar on page 24).

All of the "growing techniques" above refer to the first or main step of regrowing each of these vegetables or fruits. In many cases, to prolong the harvest, you'll transplant outside or into a larger container. Each of those details is explained in the individual plant profiles.

GROWING ON: INDOORS VERSUS OUTDOORS

There is some basic gardening information that will help you continue to regrow your kitchen scraps, whether indoors or out.

Growing Edibles: The Basics

Soil: Use soilless mix to regrow plants indoors. If you're growing outdoors, check the soil pH and make sure it isn't highly alkaline (above 8.0) or highly acidic (below 5.5). You can get pH test kits at the garden center; they are not difficult to use. It's almost always a good idea to add compost to the soil where you're planning to grow plants outside—more about compost later in this chapter. It's also a good idea to cultivate the soil to a depth of 3 to 6 inches so that it is nice and loose. Use a garden rake or a four-tine cultivator to loosen the soil.

Light: All edibles growing outdoors do best in full sun. Cool-weather leafy greens can handle some shade as the weather warms. When growing edibles indoors, think about investing in a small grow light setup for a longer-lasting, tastier harvest. There are small tabletop units, and there are units that look like bookshelves, with lights on the underside of each shelf to shine on the plants below. If you're not ready for that commitment yet, put your plants in the sunniest part of your home.

Water: Most edibles need consistent moisture. The soil should be about as damp as a wrung-out sponge, indoors or out. You may need to water more or less often than you might think to keep that consistency.

Food: If you're just regrowing some cuttings in water or soil to harvest for a bit, there's no need to fertilize. If you're trying to grow a full-season vegetable or fruit to fruition outside, you'll need to feed. Those instructions are in individual plant profiles.

Growing Outdoors versus Growing Indoors

The instructions in this book are split pretty evenly between growing plants indoors and growing plants outdoors. The reality is that some plants are simply too large to grow indoors if you want to get a harvest. If you have an entire solarium to dedicate to indoor gardening, you can create a jungle of squash vines, peanuts, potatoes, and sweet potatoes. If you have an unlimited electricity budget and a large basement, you can set up grow lights and grow all of your own food.

For the most part, though, you'll be enjoying your scraps until it's time to compost them, starting slips or transplants to plant outside, or directly planting your saved scraps (seeds) outside. Each plant profile has details describing the best course of action and enjoyment for that particular plant part.

THE END (AND THE BEGINNING): COMPOSTING

All good things eventually come to an end. There are only so many iterations of regrowing kitchen scraps before you end up with unusable parts. The lettuce bolts. The beets stop producing greens. What's next? Compost!

Compost is gold in a soil-like form. It is like duct tape in the garden, fixing almost any problem. Soil drains too fast? Add compost to retain water. Soil too heavy and slow to drain? Add compost to lighten the texture. Is rain washing beneficial nutrients out of the soil faster than they're naturally replenished? Add compost to hold on to them. In some areas, you can't even apply fertilizer to the garden without first adding compost, because the fertilizer will just wash right out of the soil.

Compost is simply organic matter (such as vegetable peels, the finished end of a turnip, egg shells, coffee grounds, shredded leaves, grass clippings, newspaper) that has been broken down by naturally occurring microbes. Because the components have been broken down by microbes—digested, if you will—plants can take up the nutrients. Adding compost to the soil is beneficial to plants in a way that adding, say, a bunch of raw carrot peels is not. Compost gives plants nutrients in a form they can use. It also feeds the existing soil microbes so they stay healthy and will break down materials that naturally end up in the garden, such as fallen leaves or twigs. Everything in the garden is interconnected, which is something that is easy to forget when you're regrowing only small parts of plants.

Buy a kitchen compost bucket or make your own.

Kitchen Compost Containers

If you're planning to truly reduce waste from the kitchen, you'll want a convenient way to collect scraps until you're ready to put them in the compost pile. A five-gallon bucket under the kitchen sink is usually the best plan of attack. Line it with newspaper and add a new layer of shredded paper on top every time you add new scraps. If you find that you aren't emptying it terribly often, you can sprinkle some charcoal into the container to keep the odor down.

Kitchen compost containers are also available for purchase. These are often ceramic or metal with tight lids. Some have vents and charcoal filters to keep odors down. These aren't expensive, but they're also not very big. Which choice is right for you depends on how many scraps you generate.

Now that you understand the basics, let's start regrowing!

Regrow Roots and Underground Stems in Soil

IIIIIIIIIIIIIIIIIIIIIIIIIIIIIIIIIIIIIII

PLANTS TO PICK

- **Potatoes**
- **Ginger**
- **Turmeric**
- **Sweet potatoes**
- **Carrots**
- **Beets**
- **Turnips**
- **Radishes**

You know those old potatoes sprouting at the bottom of the kitchen drawer? You don't have to throw them on the compost pile. You can actually cut them up and grow an entire new harvest of potatoes. How about those slightly shriveled carrots in the drawer with the potatoes—did you know you can regrow those too? You won't get another carrot, but you will get some leafy tops that are great additions to soups and salads. Plus, it is really fun to watch the carrot tops grow.

Not all vegetables that grow underground are "roots." Some are true taproots (such as carrots), some are tuberous roots (such as sweet potatoes), and still others are technically tuberous stems (such as potatoes). These parts all grow underground, so what is the difference exactly?

The main difference between the roots and stems is that tuberous stems will have eyes or buds in multiple places on the plant, while taproots and tuberous roots will only have buds or part of the stem at the top of the root—a distinction you can clearly see if you compare a potato and carrot. **This distinction is the most important thing to understand when regrowing these types of foods.**

When you're getting these plants ready to regrow, always look for the "eyes" or the growing tip, and make sure that each piece you plant has one. Otherwise, you're just burying a piece of potato that won't sprout, but instead will simply rot—suitable for compost but not regrowing.

Root your own sweet potato slips. See page 51 for instructions.

CARROTS

You won't be regrowing the root portion of the carrot, but instead the leafy greens that you can enjoy in salads, braised with a little garlic, or in soups. That's because carrots are biennial root vegetables that only produce taproots in the first year of growth. By the time you buy them in the store, they are already in their second year, so there is no way to regrow the root portion. If these roots had been left in the ground instead of being harvested, the plants would eventually send up flower stalks and produce seeds.

Some carrots are treated so that their tops don't sprout in the store—these just won't work for regrowing. So if you want to regrow your carrots, here are a few things to think about when you're shopping. Your best bet is carrots with their leaves intact. But sometimes your store doesn't offer those. In that case, search for carrots with tops that have a brownish or blackish spot on the top. That is the left-over stem. If the tops are clean-cut and orange, you won't be able to regrow them.

How to Regrow Carrots

You will need a sharp knife, a flowerpot with a diameter of at least 6 inches, soilless potting mix, and a watering can.

1. To prepare the carrots, use a knife to make a clean cut through the carrot so there is only about 1 inch left, plus the top. If the carrot has leaves on it, snip the leaves off, but be careful to leave the top of the carrot intact. (Keeping the leaves on will discourage the carrots from growing more leaves.) **a**

2. Fill the pot with soilless mix, which is sterile and less likely to have bacteria or fungi that could cause the carrot ends to rot. Water the mix so that it is about as damp as a wrung-out sponge.

3. Plant the cuttings by sticking the carrots into the soilless mix with the top ends up. Bury the carrots about half way. **b**

4. Set the flowerpot somewhere bright and sunny, and keep the soil moist but not soggy.

fun fact

Carrots are part of the parsley family, which also includes dill, fennel, parsnip, celery, and coriander. Queen Anne's lace is also a member of this plant family, and you'd recognize the resemblance if you allowed carrots, dill, or fennel to flower. They all have flat-topped flower heads made of many separate flowers on short stems that cluster together. The type of flower is called an *umbel*. If you turn the flower heads upside-down, they look like umbrellas! Both words derive from the same Latin word, *umbra*, which means "shade."

If you're lucky, your carrot tops will flower. In addition to looking beautiful, these flowers produce seeds you can harvest.

growing tip

Carrots are cool-weather vegetables. If you want to grow them outside, plant in the mid-spring or mid-fall.

Harvest and Keep Growing!

Keep the soil moist while you enjoy the harvest of the greens as they grow. You'll start seeing the tops sprout within a week or so, but it will take a few weeks to get tops big enough to eat. Snip off greens as needed.

Carrot tops are edible and perfectly delicious in place of parsley in salads, soups, and on sandwiches. Enjoy the tops for as long as the plants produce them. It is possible that the plant will send up a flower stalk, which will be lovely to look at. Once the plant flowers, you can save some seed to plant or simply compost the remains. A good way to try to get flowers if they're not coming in your pot is to plant the tops outside in a sunny spot. Keep them watered and watch for a flower stalk. If you are lucky, you may get a flower stalk or two from which you can harvest seeds. Seeds will last for up to 3 years if stored in cool, dry conditions. (A rule of thumb is 50 degrees and 50 percent humidity.)

You can dig up the entire plant and start over again with a few small pieces.

GINGER

Ginger root is expensive to buy for cooking, so why not buy once and grow your own? Ginger root comes from a tropical plant that can grow outdoors during the summer and indoors during the winter (unless you're in the virtually frost-free USDA growing zones 9 to 11, in which case you can just plant a piece of ginger root outside and let it go to town). Ginger is a flavorful addition to soups, curries, and stews. You can also use it to make tea.

We eat the *rhizome*, or underground stem, of the ginger plant. Any time you purchase a piece of ginger for cooking, you're almost guaranteed to get a piece with multiple growing tips or eyes. As with potatoes, look for organic or untreated ginger as you shop if you think you want to regrow it. You can tell if a piece of ginger is prime for resprouting because the eyes will have already started to grow a little bit at the store. Those pieces are great for no-waste gardeners.

How to Regrow Ginger

You will need a sharp knife, a flowerpot with a diameter of 6 to 12 inches, soilless potting mix, and a watering can.

1. To prepare ginger for growing, snap off or use the knife to cut 1-inch-long pieces of ginger root that have "eyes" on them. Let the pieces sit for a day or two to dry out a bit before planting. This is an important step because fresh cuts are more hospitable to bacterial and fungi, which, if allowed to infiltrate, will cause the pieces of ginger to rot before they can grow. You don't want the pieces to sit for much longer than a day or two, though, because they will completely dry out and then will not regrow as easily. (a)

2. Fill the pot with soilless mix, which is sterile and less likely to have bacteria or fungi that could cause the ginger pieces to rot. Water the mix so that it is about as damp as a wrung-out sponge. Don't let the soil stay soggy, because that can also cause the pieces to rot.

3. Plant the pieces of ginger by sticking them into the soilless mix with the eyes facing up. Cover the cut pieces with one to two inches of soil. Space pieces 3 to 4 inches apart. A 6-inch pot will fit three pieces of ginger. A 12-inch pot will fit six to eight pieces. (b)

4. Set the flowerpot somewhere bright and sunny, and wait for the pieces to grow. Once the plants have larger stems, you'll notice that the soil dries out faster, and you'll have to water more frequently.

b

Sushi is often served with pickled ginger, which has a pinkish tinge. This ginger is pickled with a mixture of sweet rice vinegar and sugar. The reaction between the sugar and vinegar is what causes the pink color.

Harvest and Keep Growing!

Three to four months after planting ginger root, when you can see some good shoots, scratch some soil aside, exposing the roots, and break off small pieces of ginger root to use. If the plant outgrows the original pot you started in, simply transplant it into a larger pot. Move the pot outside during the summer to encourage rapid growth (which means a bigger harvest, faster!).

After about a year of growth, dig up the whole plant, trim off the stems and compost them, clean off the roots to keep, and then restart the process all over again. Ginger root keeps in the refrigerator for about 2 to 3 weeks, though it loses flavor fast. You can store it in the freezer by peeling it and grating it into small piles of 1 or 2 tablespoons on a cookie sheet or in a plastic container. Stick the container in the freezer to let the piles freeze, then drop them into a plastic bag and keep them in the freezer for up to 6 months.

TURMERIC

Fresh turmeric is quite a luxury! The scent of the freshly grated root is amazing, livening up soups, salads, and, especially egg dishes. It is, however, expensive to buy and sometimes difficult to find, so why not grow your own? Turmeric has fantastic anti-inflammatory benefits, so you'll often find capsules filled with dried turmeric in the herbal remedies section of health food markets.

To grow your own, you'll start the turmeric plants indoors and then move them outside for the summer. Turmeric flowers are really pretty and worth growing for the tropical look they'll lend to the garden as much as for the edible roots.

growing tip

Turmeric will stain your hands yellowish-orange, so wear gloves when handling fresh turmeric or wash your hands and cutting surfaces immediately after you're finished cutting it.

How to Regrow Turmeric

You will need a sharp knife, a flowerpot with a diameter of at least 6 inches, soilless potting mix, and a watering can.

1. Use the sharp knife to slice a few 1-inch pieces of turmeric root. Each piece should have at least two eyes (or buds). Sometimes you can break off pieces, but turmeric can be pretty dense. It's easier to just cut it. Allow the pieces to dry out for a day or so. This will prevent bacteria and fungi from entering the cut ends.  [a]

2. Fill the pot with soilless mix. It's important to use soilless mix if you can, because it is less likely to contain bacteria and fungi that cause the pieces to rot. Water the soil so that it is about as damp as a wrung-out sponge. Take care not to let the soil get soggy. If you overwater, add some more potting mix until it is just as damp as you'd like. (You can always take some out of the pot if the pot ends up overfilled. Shoot for a 1-inch gap between the top of the soil and the top of the pot.)

3. Plant the pieces of turmeric by sticking them into the soilless mix with the eyes facing up. Cover the cut pieces with 1 to 2 inches of soil. Space pieces 3 to 4 inches apart. A 6-inch pot will fit three pieces of turmeric. A 12-inch pot will fit six to eight pieces.

4. Set the flowerpot somewhere bright and sunny, and wait for the pieces to grow. As the plants get larger, you'll need to check the soil moisture more frequently and water more often.

fun fact

Turmeric roots are used to dye everything from textiles to mustard. They lend color to cosmetics and are used in Hindu wedding ceremonies.

Harvest and Keep Growing!

I've suggested using a 6-inch pot to start your turmeric. The reason for starting small is that planting a tiny piece of root in a large pot can result in overwatering and rotting. A large pot also might take up a lot of space in your indoor garden during the winter. If you are dedicated to growing enough to harvest, you'll want to transplant the roots to a larger pot when the stems are about 6 inches tall and then move the pot outside for the summer. Turmeric will be happy outside in the same conditions you need for planting tomatoes—nighttime temperatures above 65 degrees Fahrenheit.

It takes about 8 to 9 months to grow turmeric roots large enough to use. If you start regrowing turmeric indoors in December, by the following year's frost, you'll be able to unearth a big harvest. You can regrow turmeric any time, but that is a general timeline for a big payoff.

When roots are ready for harvest, the stems of the plant may die back or turn yellow. But even if they don't turn, you can still dig up the roots within that 8- or 9-month timeframe. Trim off the old stems and compost. Wash the soil off of the roots, break them into pieces, peel them, and then store in airtight containers in the freezer. (Peeling is an optional step. The skin on turmeric isn't all that thick. It's more like a carrot than a potato in that way.) You can grate the turmeric straight from the freezer onto whatever dish you are cooking. While dense, turmeric is not as fibrous as ginger and is easier to grate. Make sure to save a few pieces from your harvest to start growing again!

If your potatoes are already sprouting like this, you know they're good to regrow!

POTATOES

Looking for a low-input, high-reward project? Grow your own potatoes! Potatoes are tuberous stems that instinctively want to regrow, provided that they have not been treated with chemicals to prevent them from sprouting. You've witnessed this if you have left a bag of potatoes sitting for too long and have seen the eye buds starting to sprout. Organic potatoes are best to regrow because they're less likely to have been treated to prevent sprouting. When you buy a bag of potatoes for cooking, set one firm potato aside for regrowing.

You can start leftover potatoes indoors and then plant them outdoors, or you can use these instructions to plant potatoes directly outside into the garden. Potatoes are generally not very well suited to growing indoors to maturity, in part because the plants get very large.

How to Regrow Potatoes

You'll need a sharp knife, isopropyl alcohol, a large pot (18 to 24 inches in diameter), potting soil, and a watering can. For sprouting potatoes to plant outside, you'll need a seedling flat and soilless mix instead of the pot and soil. For a pot this size, you'll want to plant only about two pieces.

1. Wash the potatoes, and then prepare them for planting as follows. Disinfect a sharp knife using the isopropyl alcohol. Do not skip this step, as potatoes are particularly susceptible to rotting if bacteria or fungi are introduced to the cut ends.

2. Look at the potatoes and identify the eyes, or buds. Cut each potato into 1- to 2-inch pieces, taking care to leave two eyes on each piece. a

3. Allow the cut pieces to "cure" or dry out for a few days before planting. Set them in a cool, dry place. Do not skip this step, as it helps ensure that there's no "fresh potato" to immediately be attacked by microbes in the soil. The curing process allows the potato to form a new protective skin on the cut side.

4. Fill the pot about halfway with potting soil if you're planning to grow potatoes that way. If you want to presprout potatoes for planting outside in the garden, fill a seedling flat with soilless mix. Either way, water the soil so it is about as damp as a wrung-out sponge.

5. Place the potato cuttings in the pot or the seedling flat and cover with 2 to 3 inches of soil. If you're planning to grow the potatoes in the pot, leave 6 inches between pieces. If you're just presprouting the pieces before moving them outside, you can leave 1 or 2 inches between pieces.

b

6. Set the pot or flat somewhere sunny and keep the soil moist while the plants are sprouting. When the presprouted potatoes have a few leaves, you can transplant them outside. Leave 18 inches between pieces. If you're growing potatoes in pots, gradually add more soil as the stems grow, always leaving 2 to 3 sets of leaves above the soil line. b

Harvest and Keep Growing!

Potatoes are cool-weather vegetables. If you want to grow them outside, presprout or plant in pots that you can move outside about 2 to 3 weeks before the last frost. As plants grow, you can hill up the stems to increase production. (Push the soil up around potato stems, allowing a few sets of leaves to peek out.) Water potatoes when the plants are flowering if you're not getting regular rainfall.

Harvest new potatoes 3 weeks after the plants flower by gently digging around for small tubers. Harvest the rest of the potatoes a couple of weeks after the foliage turns yellow. Dig up the potatoes and allow them to dry out for a couple of days before bringing them inside and cleaning them off. Store in a dark, cool location.

fun fact

Thomas Jefferson introduced Americans to french fries. He had encountered them while serving as the American Minister to France between 1784 and 1789. At a White House state dinner in 1802, he asked his chef to prepare the fried potatoes in the French manner, which at the time was thinly sliced and fried. They didn't take off until the early 1900s, but french fries are still one of the main ways that Americans consume potatoes today.

BEETS

Beets are having a heyday on the menu. You can't walk into a farm-to-table restaurant without encountering at least one salad prominently featuring beets. In addition to the traditional red beets, white, golden, and red-and-white-striped beets are available on grocery shelves. All can be regrown, as long as they still have their leaves or the tops of their roots intact.

Beets are biennial taproots, much like carrots, and the growing tip of a beetroot is right at the top of the root. So when you regrow beets, you're growing them for the tops, called *beet greens*, rather than the roots. Beet greens are delicious, though. Baby beet greens (they're really called that!) are almost a staple ingredient in fancy salad mixes. Larger beet greens (what you'd cut off of beets you buy at the store) are delicious when sautéed with some garlic and lemon juice.

How to Regrow Beets

You will need a sharp knife, a flowerpot with a diameter of at least 6 inches, soilless potting mix, and a watering can.

a

b

1. To prepare the beets, use a knife to make a clean cut through the beet, leaving only ¾ inch, plus the top. If the beet has leaves on it, snip the leaves off, but be careful to leave the top intact. Keeping the leaves on the top discourages more leaves from growing, but you can cook the ones you just snipped. (a) (b)

2. Fill the pot with soilless mix, which is sterile and less likely to have bacteria or fungi that could cause the beet tops to rot. Leave about an inch between the top of the soil and the edge of the pot so that when you water the soil, the soil does not float up and over the edge of the top. Water the mix so that it is about as damp as a wrung-out sponge.

growing tip

Wear gloves when handling beets or wash your hands and the countertop immediately after slicing and dicing. Red beets stain everything, and you don't want your kitchen to look like a murder scene.

3. Plant the cuttings by sticking the beet tops into the soilless mix with the top ends up. Bury the beets about halfway, leaving the tops out. For the sake of regrowing, you can leave about ½ inch to 1 inch between plant pieces. They don't need a lot of room. Ⓒ

4. Set the flowerpot somewhere bright and sunny. Keep the soil moist as the beet tops begin to sprout and grow.

Harvest and Keep Growing!

Keep beets growing as long as they produce greens. Snip young greens to use in salads or soups. Once they stop producing, throw the tops into the compost pile. You can try to plant the beet tops outside to see if they'll send up a flower stalk. One benefit if you're successful with this experiment is that pollinators love the little beet flowers. Your other vegetables will thank you.

fun fact

In addition to being a great source of antioxidants, beets are also mood boosters. The roots contain betaine, which has been used to treat depression, and tryptophan, the same compound linked to peaceful, post-Thanksgiving-turkey-dinner naps.

Plants regrow at different speeds, as evidenced by these two turnip tops "planted" at the same time.

TURNIPS

Turnips are delicious when prepared well. Large turnip roots can be roasted and mashed, like potatoes, but have more vitamins. Young turnips have a slightly sweet flavor and are actually delicious raw when sliced or grated and thrown into a salad. Turnip greens (the leafy tops) have a long history in the South, where they're cooked with ham hocks or salt pork and onions and served as part of Sunday dinner.

Turnips are taproots like carrots and beets. The technique of regrowing them is similar to other taproots, and the outcome is the same. When you regrow turnips, you'll get tasty turnip tops but not another taproot. Make sure the turnips you buy have their tops intact or else you won't be able to regrow them.

How to Regrow Turnips

You will need a sharp knife, a flowerpot with a diameter of at least 6 inches, soilless potting mix, and a watering can.

1. To prepare the turnip tops, use a knife to make a clean cut through the turnip, leaving only ¾ inch, plus the top. If the turnip has leaves on it, snip the leaves off, being careful to leave the top intact, because keeping the leaves discourages the turnip from growing new ones. You can cook these leaves! In fact, you *should* cook them, because large, mature turnip greens are fuzzy and not delicious when eaten raw. Ⓐ Ⓑ

2. Fill the pot with soilless mix, a sterile potting mix that is less likely to have fungi or bacteria in it that will cause the turnip pieces to rot. Leave about an inch between the top of the soil and the edge of the pot so that when you water the soil, it does not float up and over the edge of the top. Water the mix so that it is about as damp as a wrung-out sponge.

growing tip

Turnips are cool-weather vegetables. You're most likely to find locally grown turnips for eating (and regrowing) during the fall and early spring.

3. "Plant" the cuttings by sticking the turnip tops into the soilless mix with the top ends up. Bury the turnips about halfway, leaving the tops sticking out of the soil.

4. Set the flowerpot somewhere bright and sunny. Water the soil so that it stays evenly moist as the turnip tops begin to sprout and grow.

Harvest and Keep Growing!

Grow turnip tops for as long as they produce young leaves. While you need to cook larger turnip leaves before eating them, young leaves that are 2 inches or shorter can go in salads. When the turnips stop growing, compost them. As with beets and carrots, you can always try to regrow a few turnips outside. You might get a flower stalk!

fun fact

Turnips were the original jack-o-lanterns. Centuries ago, Celtic people in Ireland carved faces into turnips and placed candles inside the carved vegetables, lighting the way to ward off evil spirits.

RADISHES

If you buy a bunch of radishes with the tops on, you'll get more greenery than roots. Most people chop off the tops and throw them away, but they deserve a place at the table alongside other greens. They're most delicious when prepared by wilting. Melt a bit of butter in a skillet and throw the radish greens in for a couple of minutes. Remove promptly and dress with a grind of salt and a squeeze of lemon juice. For a little variety on your plate, look for watermelon radishes, which have distinctive pink and white interiors. There are also purple, yellow, white, and black radishes.

To regrow radishes, you'll follow many of the same steps used for regrowing other taproots, such as carrots and turnips. The result is similar as well. You'll get young radish greens for eating raw or cooked, but not new radishes.

How to Regrow Radishes

You will need a sharp knife, a flowerpot with a diameter of at least 6 inches, soilless potting mix, and a watering can.

1. To prepare radish tops for regrowing, use a knife to make a clean cut through the radish, leaving only ½ inch, plus the top. If the radish has leaves on it, trim or cut off the leaves, being careful to leave the top intact, because otherwise new ones won't grow. You can cook and eat radish leaves the same way you'd cook turnip greens. [a]

2. Fill the pot with soilless mix, a sterile potting mix that is less likely to have fungi or bacteria in it that will cause the radishes to rot. Leave about an inch between the top of the soil and the edge of the pot so that when you water the soil, it does not float up and over the edge of the top. Water the mix so that it is about as damp as a wrung-out sponge.

3. "Plant" the cuttings by sticking the radish tops into the soilless mix with the top ends up. Bury the radish pieces about halfway, allowing the tops to stick out of the soil. You can plant radish tops fairly close together, leaving just an inch or so between pieces. That means you can replant an entire bunch from the grocery in one pot if you want to. [b]

4. Set the flowerpot somewhere bright and sunny. Water the soil so that it stays evenly moist as the radish tops begin to sprout and grow.

Marino Branch
Brainse Marino
Tel: 8336297

growing tip

Radishes are some of the easiest vegetables to grow from seed out in the garden. Plant in the spring or late fall, and harvest when the roots are about 1 inch in diameter. Then regrow the tops. Just as if you bought the radishes at the grocery store, there's no reason to just pitch them once you eat the roots.

Harvest and Keep Growing!

The young leaves of radishes (up to about 1 inch in length) add delicious peppery flavor to salads and sandwiches. Use as a fresh garnish on soups. When the radishes stop producing leaves, compost the tops.

fun fact

In Oaxaca, Mexico, there's a festival called *Noche de Rabanos*, or "Night of the Radishes," on December 23. Radishes are specially grown for the festival, then carved starting a few days before the event. Artists stage elaborate scenes, and visitors line up for miles to view the creations.

SWEET POTATOES

Sweet potatoes are tuberous roots with eyes at the tops of the roots. Those eyes aren't always apparent, but they are there! You can regrow sweet potatoes and produce an entire harvest to eat throughout the following winter. Sweet potatoes do require a three-step process to regrow from tuber to harvest, but you'll be glad you took the time to grow your own, because you can get a huge harvest from a small investment.

Be aware that some sweet potatoes will have been treated so that they won't sprout. Buy organic or from the farmers' market when you have the chance. Grab an extra one to sprout.

Not sure how to use your bounty of sweet potatoes? They are versatile and can be cooked in almost any way. Roast them with other root vegetables and some of the rosemary you grew from cuttings (see page 116). Boil and puree them to make mashed sweet potatoes. You can make sweet potato casserole, or slice them thinly and fry them up. They taste great when prepared sweet with cinnamon or savory with herbs.

How to Regrow Sweet Potatoes

You will need a cup or jar with a mouth wide enough to fit the sweet potato, toothpicks, snips or scissors, potting soil, a seedling flat, and a watering can.

There are three main phases of growing sweet potatoes at home:

1. Rooting the sweet potato so that it produces slips, which are small plants

2. Detaching the slips from the tuber and rooting the slips

3. Planting the slips in soil

Sweet potatoes need several months to grow and produce roots large enough to harvest. Start growing your slips at least 2 to 3 months before you want to plant them outside.

Step 1: Rooting the sweet potato and producing slips

1. Place the sweet potato in the jar or cup. You need to place the root end down and the shoot (stem) end up. That is sometimes easier said than done. How do you know which is which? Often, the root end will taper and be pointier than the shoot end. Sometimes you can see some little buds sprouting at the top end, which will help you determine that it is the top.

    If the sweet potato is shorter than the cup is tall, you can stick four toothpicks into the root end of the sweet potato so that the top of it sticks out above the cup rim.

a

2. Fill the cup with water, leaving at least 2 to 3 inches of sweet potato above the water level.

3. Allow the sweet potato to grow roots and sprout little shoots. The little shoots or stems at the top are the slips. Change the water once per week or so while the shoots are sprouting. Do not let the roots dry out. This can take between 4 to 6 weeks.

You're ready to move to phase two when the little stems emerging from the top of the sweet potato are 3 to 4 inches long.

Step 2: Rooting the Slips

1. Snip or pull the slips off of the sweet potato. Each sweet potato will produce between five to fifteen slips.

2. Fill a clean glass or jar with water, and add the slips. ⓑ

3. Allow the slips to form roots. These will quickly start to develop. Plant when the roots are at least 1 inch long.

Step 3: Planting the slips

You can plant the slips in seedling flats to allow them to grow more roots before transplanting, or you can plant them outside. Plant outside when the soil has warmed up, about a month after the last frost in your area. Plant the sweet potatoes in hills or deeply cultivated soil when the weather is warm. (To make a hill, build soil up 4 to 8 inches and plant plants at the top.) Space plants 18 inches apart.

Sweet potato slips transplanted into the garden start to form tubers.

growing tip

Get a big harvest from sweet potato plants by growing them outdoors in the ground. Sweet potatoes grown in containers sometimes produce long skinny roots that circle the pot instead of plumping up.

Homegrown sweet potatoes harvested from the garden tend to be plumper than those grown in pots.

Harvest and Keep Growing!

Water as the plants are becoming established and make sure they receive at least 1 inch of water per week. Otherwise, you can just let the stems ramble and grow until early to mid-October, at which point you can carefully dig around the stem and uproot the clumps. Each slip will produce between three to eight new sweet potatoes. Cure the sweet potatoes by allowing them to sit in a warm, humid location for a week after harvesting. Then you can brush them off and store them in paper bags in the closet until you're ready to use them. The sweet potatoes will keep for 3 to 5 months. Make sure to save one for regrowing!

fun fact

Sweet potatoes can be used for more than just eating. George Washington Carver, a well-known botanist and inventor born in the 1860s (exact date unknown) and famous for his work with peanuts, also created 118 products made from sweet potatoes, including dyes, wood fillers, and library pastes (glue).

Regrow Stems and Modified Stems in Soil

||||||||||||||||||||||||||||||||||||

When you cook with green onions and leeks, don't throw the ends out! You can regrow them. They're stems, and they're some of the easiest plants to regrow. Regrowing stems makes sense because when you do, you are starting with everything you need to keep a plant going. You don't have to guess at whether the stem will grow. You just have to put the stem in an environment where it will thrive.

As discussed in Chapter 1, bulbs, including garlic, shallots, and bulbing onions, are modified stems. The growing tip is buried deeply in the center of the bulb, protected by modified leaves. Bunching onions and leeks are leaves (the parts that we eat) and stems (compressed and situated near the bottom of the plants).

These are great plants to regrow because they're so easy to tend and because you can get a pretty decent harvest from them, long-term. The basic planting method is similar for all of these plants, but the outcomes and timing vary slightly. Pay close attention to the details. All of these onion family plants except for shallots will flower and set seed eventually if left in the garden. That's one way to keep the harvest going. It takes a while to grow any of them from seed to harvest, but doing so is another fun garden project. Some of these plants are easy to regrow in water, as well.

PLANTS TO PICK

Onion family plants are excellent for this growing technique.

- Garlic
- Bulbing onions
- Shallots
- Leeks

Leeks after two weeks of regrowing.

but that yields different long-term results. Check Chapter 6 for more information on that growing technique.

(Technically, rhizomes and tuberous stems are also modified stems, but growing them is different than growing the modified stems and stems covered in this chapter. Learn how to grow them in Chapter 2.)

growing tip

Plants in the onion family are, for the most part, cool-weather plants. If you're planning to regrow or grow these plants outside, check with your local cooperative extension agency or regional gardening book for instructions about when to plant for the biggest and best harvest.

GARLIC

Can you imagine trying to cook without garlic? It would be almost impossible to end up with anything even slightly flavorful. The pungent flavor of garlic comes from a chemical reaction that occurs when the plant cells rupture. That is why whole garlic is not smelly, but minced garlic can make your eyes water. Garlic flowers, called *garlic scapes*, are edible. They usually appear in the spring as curled up stems with a swollen end (that will open to become the flower). The scapes are especially good when pickled.

Garlic from your regular grocery store has probably been treated so that it won't sprout before it can be sold. That means it might or might not sprout if you plant it. Go shopping for organic garlic or look for older cloves that have already started to sprout. (Sometimes you can find these at the grocery store or food co-op.) If you buy an entire head of garlic, you can save a few cloves (sections) for planting. For the biggest harvest, you'll want to plant the biggest bulbs.

Garlic grown inside will not get big enough to produce bulbs, so you'll eat the leaves. If you want to grow garlic heads to dry and save, you need to plant outside at some point. Consult local planting information about the right kind to plant in your area and the right time to do it. You'll almost always want to plant in the fall for a spring to early summer harvest. Elephant garlic (which is similar to garlic but not actually garlic) grows well in extremely warm climates (zones 9 to 10). Hardneck garlic grows well in cold regions, and softneck garlic grows well in warmer, temperate regions.

How to Regrow Garlic

You will need potting soil, flowerpot(s) (4 to 6 inches in diameter), a tray to catch runoff, and a watering can.

1. Separate the cloves of garlic into individual cloves. There is no need to peel them. (a)

2. Fill the container with potting soil. (Or, if you're planting garlic outside, cultivate the soil so it is nice and loose.)

3. Plant the garlic cloves 1 to 1½ inches deep, and cover with soil. You can plant cloves close together—about ½ inch apart. (If you're planting outside, choose a sunny spot, and plant the cloves about 6 inches apart.) (b)

4. Water the soil until it is about as damp as a wrung-out sponge.

5. Place the container in a bright, sunny location. Keep the soil (indoors or out) evenly moist. Indoors, you should start to see new shoots emerging fairly quickly. Outdoors, you might not see shoots sprouting for a while. Garlic planted outside will first grow roots and then, later, stems. The plants growing outdoors will grow roots and then go dormant until early spring.

fun fact

Garlic has antibiotic properties and has been used as an antiseptic and antibiotic for centuries.

Garlic that has started sprouting will not be as flavorful, so regrow it instead!

Harvest and Keep Growing!

If you're growing your garlic inside, snip off the leaves for use during cooking. They'll have a different flavor than garlic cloves and can be used like green onions. Snip as needed, and compost the bulb once it stops producing.

If you're growing outside, let the plants grow roots, and watch for new shoots in the spring. When the scapes, or flower stems, start to appear, snap them off and eat them. That way the plants will put more energy into growing big, juicy garlic bulbs.

When the leaves start to die back, you can pull up the bulbs and hang them up to dry.

growing tip

Stop watering garlic outside once the tops start to dry. At that point, the plant is nearing the end of its life cycle, and you'll want to allow it to dry out.

An onion that is already sprouting is great for regrowing.

BULBING ONIONS

Bulbing onions are the big onions with the papery skin that you use as sandwich toppers or sauté with carrots and celery for a soup base. At any given time you probably have at least one old onion at the bottom of the refrigerator drawer. It might even be starting to sprout! Those are the ones to experiment with because you know you'll get good results. They're *already* growing, so you just have to keep them growing.

Some onions are treated so that they won't sprout. If the onion you try to regrow doesn't sprout, it isn't a failure of your horticultural skills. It was probably just the onion. Compost it, and try again.

Onions are sensitive to day length (actually, sensitive to night length), so when you plant an onion outside that you've saved from cooking, you could get interesting results. You might get a new onion bulb to form and you might not, because you don't know which type of onion you're starting with.

How to Regrow Bulbing Onions

You will need potting soil, a sharp knife, isopropyl alcohol or Lysol®, flowerpot(s) (4 to 6 inches in diameter), a tray to catch runoff, and a watering can.

1. Carefully cut the sprouting onion in half, starting with the outer layers and working your way until you reach the sprouts. It is possible that you'll have two or three different small plants. ⓐ ⓑ

2. Fill the container with potting soil. (Or, if you're planting onions outside, cultivate the soil so that it is nice and loose.)

3. Plant the pieces of onion about 2 inches apart. Bury the roots and the plant about 1 inch deep, leaving the sprouting part or the top of the growing tip exposed. (If planting outside, choose a sunny spot.) ⓒ

4. Water the soil until it is about as damp as a wrung-out sponge.

5. Place the container in a bright, sunny location. Keep the soil (indoors or out) evenly moist. Indoors you should start to see new shoots emerging fairly quickly.

Harvest and Keep Growing!

Grow bulbing onions inside and snip off the fragrant leaves for cooking. You can also regrow onions outside, and you might get additional big bulbs to harvest that you can use and then continue to regrow. Plant outside and allow them to grow until their tops start to turn brown and fall over. At that point, you can pull the onions up and allow them to cure outside. Then store them inside in a cool, dry place.

If you're planning to store bulbing onions after growing them outside, you'll need to let them cure before bringing them in.

growing tip

Keep onions weeded and watered when growing outside. They do not grow deep roots, so they can dry out quickly and do not appreciate competition from weeds.

SHALLOTS

Shallots are part of the onion family, but they have a milder taste than most onions or garlic. They're popular in French cooking and add great flavor to salad dressings. In Asian cuisine, they are sometimes served fried or pickled.

You can see the "cloves" inside a shallot head cut in half.

Shallots grow like garlic, with many little cloves inside one head. They take a while to develop new cloves or bulbs, but you can regrow them indoors for flavorful leaves if you want results quickly.

How to Regrow Shallots

You will need potting soil, flowerpot(s) (4 to 6 inches in diameter), a tray to catch runoff, and a watering can.

1. Split apart the head of your shallot and save the biggest cloves for planting.  ⓐ

2. Fill the container with potting soil. (Or, if you're planting shallots outside, cultivate the soil so that it is nice and loose.)

3. Plant the shallot cloves or bulbs 1 to 1½ inches deep, 1 to 2 inches apart, and cover with soil. (If planting outside, choose a sunny spot.) ⓑ

4. Water the soil until it is about as damp as a wrung-out sponge. Shallots planted outside will first grow roots and then, later, stems. If planted in the fall, they may experience some start-stop-start-stop growing, but they'll start forming bulbs in the spring.

5. Place the container in a bright, sunny location. Keep the soil (indoors or out) evenly moist. Indoors, you should start to see new shoots emerging fairly quickly.

b

fun fact

Shallots give the traditional béarnaise sauce its flavor.

Shallots sprouting after a few weeks on a kitchen countertop.

Harvest and Keep Growing!

Snip off leaves of plants growing indoors to use while cooking. They can be used just like green onions.

Plant shallots outside in the fall in warmer areas (areas that do not experience months of hard freezes) and in the spring in cooler areas. Water well when first planting, and then again during dry periods.

You can start harvesting and pulling up the plants to dry when the bulbs are 2 inches in diameter. Pull them up and set them somewhere dry to cure, just like you'd cure onions.

growing tip

Shallots start forming those nice, juicy bulbs that you want to use for cooking when the days start to lengthen. If you plant them in the fall, they'll grow, but they won't be ready to harvest until the spring.

If you buy leeks with the roots cut off, they are unlikely to regrow, so look for intact roots like these.

LEEKS

I love leeks! My interest started when I lived in Vermont and frequented a restaurant that served wonderful potato leek soup. Then I moved to the middle of nowhere in upstate New York, and I had to learn to cook anything I wanted to eat, including potato leek soup. Turns out, leeks are easy to grow and fun to cook with.

Leeks are part of the onion family and, like most other family members, have a compressed growing tip surrounded by edible leaves. If you want to regrow leeks, purchase them with the roots still attached to the bottom. If the bottoms are cut off of the leeks, chances are good that the growing tips have been cut off as well.

These leeks are prepared for regrowing in water.

Leeks are amazingly easy to grow, indoors or out. The instructions here are for regrowing in soil, but you can also regrow them in water. To do that, mimic the instructions for growing green onions in water, which you'll find on page 110. Both methods work well. Leeks seem to grow slightly faster in soil than in water, but if you don't want to deal with the mess of soil, you can regrow in water instead. What you get when you regrow them depends on how big the leeks are when you plant them. If you've purchased smaller leeks (about the diameter of your finger), you can plant the leeks outside or inside and let them regrow until they have some size on them. Big, fat, leeks are fun to harvest for soups, the grill, and more. If the leeks were already large when you purchased them, you might just get a few highly flavorful green leaves to harvest.

How to Regrow Leeks

You will need potting soil, a sharp knife, isopropyl alcohol or Lysol®, flowerpot(s) (4 to 6 inches in diameter), tray to catch runoff, and a watering can.

a

1. Cut the tops off your leeks, leaving 2 to 3 inches attached to the roots. (a)

2. Fill the container with potting soil. (Or, if you're planting leeks outside, cultivate the soil so that it is nice and loose.)

3. Plant the leeks so that just about ½ inch of the plant sticks up out of the soil. You can plant them pretty close together in pots. (If planting outside, choose a sunny spot and leave 4 to 6 inches between plants.) (b)

4. Water the soil until it is about as damp as a wrung-out sponge.

5. Place the container in a bright, sunny location. Keep the soil (indoors or out) evenly moist.

fun fact

The Roman emperor Nero consumed so many leeks that he was nicknamed "The Leek Eater."

growing tip

You can harvest leeks whenever you want. The longer they grow, the more you'll have to cook with, but you can still cook with skinny leeks.

b

Harvest and Keep Growing!

You can use young leek leaves for cooking in much the same way you'd use green onions. Chop them up to add flavor to salads, soups, dips, and more.

If you plant leeks outside, you can allow them to grow throughout the cool weather. They'll really get some size on them and can be harvested for use in soups or frittatas and more. Keep the area where leeks grow evenly moist and weed-free. Push the soil up around them (this is called *hilling*) to get nice, thick, white stems for cooking.

When leeks are growing, they sometimes get soil or sand particles trapped between the layers. The best way to make sure your soup isn't crunchy is to cut the leeks in half lengthwise, and then cut them crosswise so that you have lots of small pieces. Rinse them well in a colander, really tossing the leeks and rinsing to make sure you get all of the dirt out.

Grow Seeds in Soil and Water

|||||||||||||||||||||||||||||||||||

Growing seeds is the most natural of gardening activities, but not necessarily what you might think about when regrowing kitchen scraps. You *can* save the seeds from kitchen scraps, though, and grow them into either a fruitful harvest or an interesting curiosity. There's one type of seed you'll grow primarily in water, or grow in water to get started—the avocado. Everything else you'll grow in soil.

Seeds have everything inside them needed to grow a new plant. They are the only kitchen scraps that are a one-stop shop.

What you get when you plant seeds saved from cooking depends on the plant they came from. Not all seeds that you save will produce a fruit identical to its parent; many garden plants are hybrids of two parent varieties, and the seeds they produce may revert to the genetic heritage of one of those parents. But that shouldn't discourage you from experimenting!

There's a lot of fun to be had with seeds, but some seeds have unique requirements. They may need to be shelled, cracked, stratified (that is, undergo a cold, moist period), or fermented and dried. There are specific instructions for preparing each type of seed in the individual plant profiles that follow.

Start avocado seeds in water before planting them in soil. See page 99 for instructions.

PLANTS TO PICK

- **Microgreens**
- **Pumpkins and winter squash**
- **Citrus**
- **Tomatoes**
- **Melons**
- **Peppers**
- **Fruit trees**
- **Avocados**

Microgreens are one step beyond sprouts.

MICROGREENS

You've heard of sprouts. Now get ready for microgreens! Each of these plants can be eaten as sprouts, but for an even more nutritious—and, quite frankly, pretty—addition to salads, sandwiches, soups, and for use as a garnish, grow beyond the sprout stage. Microgreens are simply seeds that were planted in soil rather than sprouted in a jar or bag. This allows the plants to grow a bit. When you eat sprouts, you're eating the "seed leaves" that are inside the seed before it sprouts. Microgreens have grown more to the point where they have one set of "true leaves" or the first leaves that grow after the seed leaves. Microgreens are more nutritionally dense than sprouts.

Here are some good seeds to grow as microgreens:

- Coriander
- Fennel
- Lentils

- Mustard
- Sesame
- Sunflowers

Lentils and sunflowers are the least expensive seed to purchase for growing as microgreens. When you're making lentil soup, simply save a handful of the dried lentils for planting. Sunflower seeds are a popular ingredient for trail mix. Buy raw shelled seed if you want to save some for regrowing. If you get really into microgreens, black-oil sunflower seed available at bird-feeding stores is cost-effective, but you're unlikely to just have that type on hand for cooking.

Look to your spice rack for herb seeds such as coriander, fennel, mustard, and (untoasted) sesame. Seeds have different viability times. Some seeds can survive for longer than others without being planted. The main point of dried herbs is not for growing but for cooking, so when raiding the spice rack for microgreen seeds, it's useful to do a germination test to see whether the seeds will sprout before you sow a full flat. (See instructions for doing a germination test on page 24.) If you do a test and they don't sprout, the seeds are just older and past viability. Then you know not to waste part of a bottle of herbs by planting them. However, you might find you have some that will grow, and that's worth the effort!

How to Grow Microgreens

You will need potting mix, a seedling flat or plastic storage container with holes in the bottom of it, a saucer or tray to catch runoff, plastic wrap or a plastic dome to fit over the container, and a watering can.

1. Fill the seedling flat or Tupperware with potting mix. [a]

2. Sow the seeds. When sowing microgreens, you'll want to scatter seeds thickly on the surface of the soil.

3. Barely cover the seeds with just a dusting of potting soil. [a]

4. Water the soil until it's just a little more damp than a wrung-out sponge. The water will help the outer layer of the seed (the seed coat) swell and signal to the plant that it is time to grow.

5. Cover the pot or seed tray with the plastic dome or plastic wrap to keep the environment moist. ⓑ

6. Place the tray or pot in a warm environment with bright, indirect light.

7. Check the soil moisture periodically. Make sure that it is staying evenly moist, but not soggy.

8. Remove the dome once the microgreens have started sprouting.

Microgreens are a one-and-done crop. They will not regrow after you snip them.

Harvest!

Harvest microgreens when the little plants have two or three sets of "true leaves." Depending on the plant, it will look like the plant has three or four sets of leaves. Usually the seed leaves shrivel once the plant begins growing true leaves, but not always. Use scissors to snip off the shoots at the soil line. You can replant in the same soil or compost the soil. But this is the end of the line for these plants.

Microgreens are tasty additions to salads, sandwiches, wraps, and soups, and also work as garnishes. The baby greens will have similar flavor to the "grown up" plants, though usually slightly milder.

Save the seeds from your Halloween pumpkins.

PUMPKINS AND WINTER SQUASH

Carving pumpkins is a basic fall tradition. Enjoying unusual decorative squash, bumpy pumpkins, and warty gourds is part of cool-weather decorating too. When I was a kid, my dad helped us with the carving part, and my mom cleaned and roasted the pumpkin seeds for us to enjoy when we were done. Yum! What if you saved a few pumpkin seeds to sprout? Many a gardener has visited the compost pile in the spring and found a big vine sprouting where they threw the jack-o-lantern after Halloween. You can decide where you want to plant your pumpkins or gourds if you clean the seeds and plant them yourself.

Plants in the squash family, including cucumbers, pumpkins, winter squash, and gourds, freely cross-pollinate with each other. What you get when you plant seeds from your squash depends on how the plant that you ate (or carved) was grown. If it was in a field with thousands of the same type, you'll probably get a pumpkin or squash that looks like the one you originally bought. If it was grown among a mixture of squash plants, you could end up with something pretty interesting. But that's no reason not to try!

How to Grow Pumpkins and Winter Squash

You'll need a garden fork and at least 4 feet by 12 linear feet of space outside to grow pumpkins (pumpkin vines are really too large to grow indoors). That amount is sufficient for about six to nine seeds. Plant pumpkins when the soil is good and warm. You can plant at the same time you plant tomatoes. Or, for true fall pumpkins, plant in June or July.

1. Use the garden fork or cultivator to cultivate the soil where you're planting the pumpkins.

2. On top of the cultivated soil, build a 6-inch-tall hill of soil.

3. Plant three or four seeds at the top of the hill, leaving 2 to 3 inches between seeds. Hill spacing depends on the variety you are growing, which you might not know since you saved the seeds. If you end up with too many vines, just pull some out!

4. Water well at the time of planting.

5. Check the soil moisture periodically. Make sure that it is staying evenly moist, but not soggy.

6. Fertilize with a balanced fertilizer (10-10-10 or 7-7-7) once per month while plants are growing.

Harvest and Keep Growing!

When is my pumpkin ready to pick? Isn't that the age-old question? It is a myth that pumpkins have to go through a frost in order to ripen. In fact, a hard frost will turn pumpkins and squash into a pile of mush. Pumpkins are ready when the rind is hard and uniformly colored. For spotted and warty pumpkins, this can prove to be a challenging assessment. Just look for a hard rind to know when to pick.

fun fact

Pumpkin flowers are edible!

These pumpkins are still somewhat shiny, so they are not quite ready to pick.

Winter squashes should have hard rinds that are somewhat dull rather than shiny. Immature, unripe fruits will be shinier, so pay attention to the fruits. If they start to get progressively less shiny you'll know you're close to having ripe fruits to pick.

Store pumpkins and winter squash in dark, cool, dry areas. Save seeds to prolong your squash experiment.

growing tip

Pumpkins do not need to experience a frost in order to be ripe. Pick them as soon as their rinds are dull.

Citrus trees are evergreen, with fragrant flowers and flavorful fruit.

CITRUS

Lemon, lime, and tangerine plants are fun to grow indoors. They'll even flower and produce fruit inside, unlike many other fruit plants. Also, they don't have to be huge in order to produce fruit. They're really great plants for the home. Most citrus that we buy come from grafted fruit trees. The top of the tree is a cutting from a known variety that is spliced together with a rootstock from a different citrus tree.

The top (called the *scion*) is likely from a hybrid plant. Oranges, lemons, limes, and grapefruits are the result of hybrid crosses between different species. The different types are maintained by vegetative propagation of the cuttings that become the tops of the scions. That means that when you save seeds from, say, a Meyer lemon, and plant it, you'll get a citrus plant, but you won't necessarily get a Meyer lemon. The fruit might be edible or it might be too sour or bitter, but it will still be fun to grow. If you can get your hands on a true Satsuma tangerine, that is your best bet for getting a citrus plant that bears fruit most similar to the one you ate.

The graft union is the place where the scion meets the rootstock. When first spliced together, the graft union is wrapped up tightly, as pictured.

Take care not to cut the seeds in half if you want to regrow them. One of these seeds has been ruined, but the rest are useable.

How to Grow Citrus

You will need potting mix, a flowerpot, saucer to fit under the flowerpot, plastic wrap or a plastic dome, and a watering can.

To save seeds from citrus, remove them from the fruit and wash away the pulpy remains of the fruit until you have clean seeds. If you want to store the seeds before planting, place them between a couple of wet paper towels and store in a plastic bag or plastic container in the refrigerator. If the seeds dry out, they won't germinate as well.

1. Fill the pot with potting soil.

2. Plant at least three seeds in the pot.

3. Cover the seeds with an inch of soil.

4. Water the soil so that it just a little more damp than a wrung-out sponge. The water will help the outer layer of the seed (the seed coat) swell, which is a signal to the plant that it is time to grow.

fun fact

Grapefruits are hybrids between the sweet orange and the pomelo, two distinctly different types of citrus. Ruby Red was the first successful commercial variety of red grapefruit.

5. Cover the pot or seed tray with the plastic dome or plastic wrap to keep the environment moist. (If seeds are outside and uncovered, you're just going to have to watch them to make sure that the soil stays moist while the seeds are germinating.) [a]

6. Place the tray or pot in a warm environment with bright, indirect light.

7. Check the soil moisture periodically. Make sure that it is staying evenly moist, but not soggy.

8. Remove the cover once the seeds have started to sprout.

Harvest and Keep Growing!

If you got your citrus to sprout, now you just have to keep it growing. You won't get flowers and fruit right away. It might take 4 or 5 years for the plant to flower. While you're waiting, grow it in bright, indirect sunlight. (A west- or south-facing window is a good spot.) Keep the soil about as damp as a wrung-out sponge. Fertilize with citrus fertilizer while the plant is actively growing. (You can tell if it is growing because it will be sprouting new, lighter-green leaves.)

Always move citrus plants outside during the summer. Plants growing inside can get stressed and overcome with spider mites and scale. Setting the pot outside during the summer allows natural predators to take care of the problem. Harden off the plants by keeping them in a shady, protected area for a week or so. You

Citrus tree growing indoors.

can move plants into a sunnier location after that, so long as they are protected from the wind. Keep the soil evenly moist. Bring plants inside before temperatures drop below 40 degrees Fahrenheit. Pot into the next sized container every other spring to account for new growth. Simply choose a pot that is 4 to 6 inches wider in diameter than the previous pot. Add some potting soil to the bottom, and then place the plant rootball in the pot. Fill around with soil. Make sure that the top of the plant rootball stays at the top of the pot (about 1 inch below the lip). Don't bury the rootball under several inches of soil.

How do you know when citrus is ripe to pick? Well, it will be hard to tell because who knows what you'll end up getting when you plant the seed. You can make some guesses by looking up the type of plant that the seed came from and picking and testing. You're not going to poison yourself, but the fruit might be more sour than you were expecting. However, the fully ripe fruit might be more sour than the one you saved seeds from anyway.

growing tip

It is worth it to invest in a citrus-specific fertilizer. Citrus have a particular fertilizing schedule, which will be listed on the fertilizer package, and particular food requirements, and those fertilizers are specially formulated just for citrus.

Nothing tastes better than a homegrown tomato.

TOMATOES

The same caveats I described for pumpkins and citrus regarding hybrid versus open-pollinated seeds also apply to tomatoes. If you purchase heirloom tomatoes, they are much more likely to be open-pollinated and produce viable seed that will result in a similar fruit to the one you ate. There aren't ironclad regulations about labeling heirlooms, so it is possible that you would purchase a box of smaller "heirloom tomatoes" that are anything but.

If you do grow healthy open-pollinated tomatoes for cooking or you purchase some at the market, it's fun to save your own seeds. If you eat a particularly delicious unlabeled variety, saving seeds is a way to try to enjoy the flavors again. You will need to ferment the tomato seeds to remove the pulp and disable any germination-inhibition effects of the fruit pulp on the seeds.

How to Grow Tomatoes

You will need potting mix, a seedling flat or flowerpot, saucer, plastic dome or plastic wrap, stakes or cages, and twine or twist ties.

1. Fill the seedling flat or pot with potting soil.

2. Sow two seeds in each cell of the seedling flat or plant groups of two seeds at least 3 inches apart in the flowerpot.

3. Cover the seeds lightly with soil.

4. Water the soil so that it is just a little more damp than a wrung-out sponge. The water will help the outer layer of the seed (the seed coat) swell, which is a signal to the plant that it is time to grow.

5. Cover the pot or seed tray with the plastic dome or plastic wrap to keep the environment moist.

6. Place the tray or pot in a warm environment with bright, indirect light. If you have a growing light setup, even better.

7. Remove the cover or dome once the plants have sprouted. a

8. Check the soil moisture periodically. Make sure that it is staying evenly moist, but not soggy.

9. Allow the plants to grow at least three to four sets of true leaves. At that point you can harden them off and transplant out into the garden.

fun fact

The wild ancestor of a tomato is a vining plant from Peru known to botanists as *Solanum pimpinellifolium*, or simply "pimp." It produces a fruit about the size of shelled pea.

GROW SEEDS IN SOIL AND WATER

HOW TO CLEAN FRUIT SEEDS BY FERMENTING THEM

a

b

To make sure that seeds are clean before planting so that they don't rot (sugar in the fruit can attract bacterial and fungi), you must ferment them. This process is used for tomatoes, eggplants, and squash.

You will need a sieve or strainer, a glass jar or bowl, a spoon, and paper towels or a drying screen.

1. Scoop seeds out of the fruit (or squeeze seeds out of the fruit). Make sure there is some pulp with the seeds. ⓐ

2. Place the seeds and pulp in a clean container with a lid and allow them to sit for 2 or 3 days. ⓑ

3. Stir the seeds daily.

4. Add a couple tablespoons of water to the jar and gently agitate the contents.

5. Pour off the fruit and pulp that float to the top of the container. The seeds will sink to the bottom.

c

Tomato seeds are tiny.

6. Wash the seeds with clean water and a sieve. ⓒ

7. Spread the seeds out on clean towels or dry paper towels to dry for at least
7 days.

Once seeds have fermented, you can spread them out on a screen to dry. Stir the
drying seeds once per day. After they are dry, you can store them in a clean, dry
plastic bag or glass container.

growing tip

Sometimes the fermented pulp will congeal into a solid mass. When you
add water, this mass will float to the top, and you can just pull it off and
throw it away. It feels a little like snot.

Harvest and Keep Growing!

Plant tomatoes outside when nighttime temperatures are at least 70 degrees Fahrenheit. They like it warm! Stake or cage indeterminate varieties. (You'll know if that is what you're growing because the indeterminate plants will become huge. Determinate, or bush, tomatoes are bred to grow only to a certain size, usually around 4 feet.) Fertilize with tomato-specific fertilizer throughout the growing season.

Tomatoes are ripe when they've reached the expected color for the variety you're growing. If you're getting unusual results in terms of fruit color, you can always taste test!

Save some seeds from the yummiest tomatoes so you can replant next year.

growing tip

When you transplant tomatoes outside, strip off all but the top pair of leaves and plant the plants deep, leaving only the top two leaves out of the ground.

You can save seeds from melons to regrow just like you save seeds from pumpkins and winter squash, but you have to ferment melon seeds much like you would with tomato seeds in order to clean the fruit off of them.

MELONS

Melons are in the same family as pumpkins and winter squash. They are often hybrids, and they freely cross-pollinate, so growing a seed from a melon that you purchase is a "choose your own adventure" situation. As with everything else, it's fun to grow the plants when you have space, if only to see what they produce. Mutant melons? Sign me up!

You have to clean the fruity pulp off of the melon seeds by fermenting before planting them, just as you did with tomato seeds (see the instructions on pages 86–87). When you ferment melon seeds, you usually need to add a bit of water to the mixture at the beginning in order for there to be enough liquid to ferment. Melon fruit is not as liquidy as tomato fruit.

How to Grow Melons

You'll need a garden fork and at least 4 feet by 12 linear feet of space outside to grow melons. (Melon vines are too large to grow indoors.) You can fit four to eight seeds in this amount of space. Plant melons when the soil is good and warm. You can plant at the same time you plant tomatoes.

1. Use the garden fork or cultivator to cultivate the soil where you're planting the melons.

2. On top of the cultivated soil, build a 6-inch-tall hill of soil.

3. Plant three or four seeds at the top of the hill, leaving 2 to 3 inches between seeds. Hill spacing depends on the variety you are growing, which you might not know since you saved the seeds from a grocery store melon. If you end up with too many vines, just pull some out!

4. Water well at the time of planting.

5. Check the soil moisture periodically. Make sure that it is staying evenly moist, but not soggy.

6. Fertilize once per month while plants are growing. a

fun fact

Cantaloupes are sometimes called "musk melons," due to their strong scent when ripe.

Melon plants are large and long. Give them plenty of space in the garden to scramble.

Harvest and Keep Growing!

When you plant melon seeds, you're going to get some sort of interesting result. The best way to guess when the fruits are ready to harvest is to know what the parent plant was and look up "days to harvest" for that plant. If you have lots of little melon fruits forming, you can also periodically pick one and taste it. There's no telling what you're getting when you plant a melon seed, so it might be tasty and it might not be—but if it turns out that it tastes bad, at least you had some practice growing.

growing tip

Cantaloupe melons are ready to harvest when their skins have turned a light tan under the network of veins on the outside of the melons.

PEPPERS

There are hundreds of different varieties of peppers, but they are all from the same species, *Capsicum annuum*. The plants have been domesticated over hundreds and hundreds of years. Pepper plants have been used for a variety of medicinal purposes. They're quite versatile in the kitchen too.

There are spicy peppers and sweet peppers. One of the most popular types of peppers, the green pepper, is picked when the fruits are not fully ripe and their seeds are not fully mature. In fact, most of the peppers you'd buy at the store are not ripe or mature enough to save and use their seeds. Your best bet for saving pepper seeds is to grow your own peppers from a seed packet or seedling transplants and leave a few fruits on the plant until they are fully ripe and almost wrinkled. At that point you can remove the seeds and spread them on a paper towel to dry.

How to Grow Peppers

You will need potting mix, a seedling flat or flowerpot, saucer, plastic dome or plastic wrap, stakes or cages, and twine or twist ties.

Plant peppers outside when nighttime temperatures are consistently above 70 degrees Fahrenheit. They like it hot!

1. Fill the seedling flat or pot with potting soil.

2. Sow two seeds in each cell of the seedling flat or plant groups of two seeds at least 3 inches apart in the flowerpot.

3. Cover the seeds lightly with soil.

4. Water the soil so that it just a little more damp than a wrung-out sponge. The water will help the outer layer of the seed (the seed coat) swell, which is a signal to the plant that it is time to grow.

5. Cover the pot or seed tray with the plastic dome or plastic wrap to keep the environment moist.

6. Place the tray or pot in a warm environment with bright, indirect light. If you have a growing light setup, even better.

7. Remove the cover or dome once the plants have sprouted. [a]

8. Check the soil moisture periodically. Make sure that it is staying evenly moist, but not soggy.

9. Allow the plants to grow at least three to four sets of true leaves. At that point you can harden them off and transplant out into the garden.

Harvest and Keep Growing!

Peppers ready to harvest and peppers ready to eat are two different things. Pretty much any pepper can be picked and eaten green, but it might have a bitter taste. Remember or make a note of what color the peppers are supposed to be when ripe, and pick them at that point.

Peppers are mature and ready to harvest for seed-saving when their skins are a bit wrinkly.

fun fact

The Scoville scale is used to indicate the hotness of the pepper. It measures the concentration of heat-producing chemicals in the pepper from 0 (bell peppers) to 3,200,000 (Carolina Reapers and Dragon's Breath peppers). Yowch!

growing tip

When handling hot peppers, wear gloves and avoid touching your eyes. I have been reminded of this tip the hard way. Several times.

Young apple tree bearing fruit.

FRUIT TREE SEEDS

Some seeds require a cold, moist treatment called *stratification*. That's what would happen in the wild if the seeds fell to the ground in fall, sat on the ground during a cold, moist winter, and sprouted in the spring.

Other seeds require *scarification*, or nicking of the seed coat. That is what would happen if a seed was eaten by an animal, then traveled through its digestive tract, and came out the other end. Ahem! The acids in the animal's stomach would break down some of the seed coat. Instead, you do that for the seed by clipping the seed coat or filing a little nick out of it.

Fruit trees, for the most part, require one or both of these types of treatment.

Apple and Pear Seeds

Apples and pears, like citrus fruits, are the products of grafted trees, so the seeds from a Granny Smith apple won't germinate and produce a Granny Smith apple. It will still produce an apple, though!

Seeds from apples and pears are easy to harvest. Just pry them out of the fruits and clean any clinging fruit pulp off of them. Wash and dry them. Set them aside in a cool, dry place until January or February.

Before they'll sprout, the seeds have to undergo stratification. This mimics what happens to the fruits in nature. Apples fall off the trees, lie on the ground, and sit through a winter. Or the fruit and seeds get eaten by an animal, then seeds are excreted and lay on the ground during the winter. Either way, it is the cold, moist period that allows the seeds to sprout. Here's how to mimic that at home. You'll need some peat moss, which you can get from a garden center, or shredded paper towels, and a glass jar.

1. Mix the seeds with peat moss or shredded paper towels and a bit of water until the mixture is barely moist (about as moist as a wrung-out sponge).

2. Place the lid over the jar and place the jar in the refrigerator.

3. Leave the seeds in the refrigerator for at least 2 months or until after the last frost in the spring.

They are then ready to plant! All fruit trees need full sun and moist, well-drained soil of a slightly acidic pH. If you're going to grow your plant outside, you can start it in a pot and then transplant it into the ground when it is 2 to 3 feet tall.

Stone Fruit Seeds

Stone fruits, such as cherries, peaches, nectarines, and plums, also require a cold, moist period in order to germinate. In addition, they have hard outer coatings that need to be cracked for faster germination. After giving the seeds their cold, moist treatment as described for apples and pears above, but before planting, use a nutcracker to gently crack the outer coating. Be careful not to completely squash the seed, which will squash the embryo on the inside and result in less than stellar germination.

You'll have to use a nutcracker to crack the hard outer pit of the peach seed.

How to Grow Fruit Tree Seeds

You will need a potting mix, flowerpot, saucer, nutcracker, and watering can.

1. Plant the seed and stratify it. Stratification is the cold, moist treatment that helps break the seed dormancy and prompts it to sprout (see page 96).

2. Continue to monitor soil moisture while the seed is germinating. Do not let the soil completely dry out at any time while the seed is germinating.

3. Grow in a pot until the plant is at least 6 inches tall. You'll get best results if you grow the fruit trees outside, rather than inside.

Harvest and Keep Growing!

Once your fruit tree is at least 6 inches tall, you should plant it outside. All fruit trees need well-drained soil and at least 6 to 8 hours of sunlight per day.

Fruit trees have pretty specific requirements to keep insect and disease problems at bay. Look up more information about the specific type of tree you're growing if you plan to try to grow the plant to maturity.

It can take years and years for a seed-grown fruit tree to flower or produce fruit. Then you don't know what you're going to get. Just keep the tree growing and enjoy the flowers when they appear—and try the fruits if they grow. Your return on growing an apple tree from seed is to be able to point to it and say, "I grew that from seed!"

fun fact

Fruit trees native to tropical areas tend to be evergreen, while those from colder climates are deciduous.

growing tip

Most fruit trees require another tree to cross-pollinate in order to get fruit. The cross-pollinating trees must bloom at the same time. This is yet another complicating factor to getting fruit from seeds that you saved. There are a handful that don't require this—try nectarines, peaches, or sour cherries.

AVOCADO

Avocado trees growing in commercial groves are, like citrus, apple, and other fruit trees, grafted plants. The top is a known variety, and the bottom is a rootstock. As with citrus, growing an avocado from seed is more of a fun experiment in growing your own cool houseplant than it is a way to guarantee an endless supply of avocadoes.

Avocados do not grow in temperatures lower than 20 degrees Fahrenheit, and those are the more cold-hardy varieties. Plants require anywhere from 5 to 15 years to produce fruit. They also do best when they have a cross-pollinator, which means you'd need two avocado plants. Where are you going to put two fully grown trees inside your house? Unless you're lucky enough to have a fairly large greenhouse, you won't have enough space to grow the trees to blooming maturity. Then, even if you raised two avocado trees from pits, the trees might not bloom at the same time, they might not bloom at all, or they might not be compatible, so you still might not get fruit.

Long story short, grow avocado pits for fun, not fruit. Here's how.

How to Grow an Avocado Pit

You will need a sponge with a plastic scrubby side, three or four toothpicks, a glass or sturdy plastic cup or bulb jar, water, and, eventually, a flowerpot, potting soil, and a saucer to catch runoff.

a

b

1. Clean the avocado seed. It should be fairly easy to just run the seed under water and gently remove the pulp from around it. If you need to, you can use the scrubby side of a plastic sponge to remove any sticky bits. [a]

2. Identify the top and bottom of the seed. The bottom part of the seed will usually be a bit broader than the top part of the seed. Sometimes the top is pointy. (If you think about this ahead of time, you can mark the top of the seed by making a scratch on the top of the seed before you take it out of the fruit because it's easier to tell which side of the fruit is the top.)

3. Stick the three or four toothpicks into the avocado pit at about mid-level in the pit. They should be evenly spaced. These toothpicks are what will hold the pit at a steady spot in the glass. [b]

4. Fill the glass with room-temperature water. The water should come just about to the top of the glass—any size of glass will work for this.

5. Place the avocado pit/toothpick assembly on the glass so that the bottom of the pit is submerged in water.

6. Set the glass somewhere warm but not in direct sunlight. Change the water once a week or so, just to keep it fresh and prevent bacteria and fungi from growing. Make sure the water that you use to refill the glass is at room temperature. ⓒ

ⓒ

Keep Growing!

The avocado pit will sprout a taproot from the bottom of the seed and a shoot (stem) from the top. You'll know that the stem is about to emerge when you see the top of the seed start to crack. Never let the taproot or bottom of the seed dry out while it is growing in water.

Once you start to see a shoot emerging, you can move the plant to an area with more light.

When the plant is between 6 to 12 inches tall, plant it in a 12-inch diameter flowerpot. Leave the top of the seed exposed. Do not cover entire seed with soil.

Keep the soil about as moist as a wrung-out sponge and give the plant as much natural sunlight as possible. You can move the plant outdoors during the summer. Just make sure to leave it in a protected location for a few days to harden it off before moving it into a more exposed area.

To keep the plant houseplant-sized and not avocado grove-sized, trim the plant back by half when it is between 12 to 18 inches tall. This will promote side shoots to grow. You can tip prune to maintain size. When the plant has outgrown your space and pruning affects the aesthetics, simply start a new pit and begin again!

growing tip

Do not let the avocado pit dry out. Start the rooting process immediately after removing the pit from the fruit or wrap it in a wet paper towel and store in a container on your counter until you can get to it.

CHAPTER

5

Regrow Whole Plants and Stems in Water

||||||||||||||||||||||||||||||||||||||

PLANTS TO PICK

Want to extend the life of that head of romaine lettuce you bought for dinner? Regrow it! You can reroot some types of plants in water just like you can reroot them in soil. Some plants root equally well both ways, while others prefer one of the two methods One advantage to rerooting in water is that it's easy to check the progress of the roots, either by simply pulling them out of the container for inspection or by using clear glass or plastic containers where the roots are visible. Regrowing in water is less messy than regrowing in soil too.

PLANTS TO PICK

- **Lettuce (and heading vegetables such as napa cabbage)**
- **Celery**
- **Green onions**
- **Fennel**
- **Lemongrass**
- **Herb stem cuttings**
- **Pineapple**

Once the plants grow roots, you can transplant into soil or simply harvest what the plant produces until it is finished. Some plants are worth the effort to keep growing in the soil, while for others it's more practical to harvest for a short time while they are rooted in water, then send them to the compost heap when the harvest is exhausted. For example, you can reroot leeks in water and get some more size on the plants for a second harvest. Lettuce, on the other hand, often results in a handful of new leaves, but it bolts (sends up flower stalks) fairly quickly and is then ready to discard.

The good part about this technique is that, for most plants, it requires little effort, so a small reward is worth the time. Here's how to do it.

From left to right, lettuce, sweet potato slips, and celery in water. Lettuce and celery are whole plants that are easy to regrow.

REGROW WHOLE PLANTS AND STEMS IN WATER

||||||||||||||||||||||||

103

Don't throw out the bottom of that head of lettuce. Stick it in water and regrow it!

LETTUCE

Head lettuces are easy to regrow. Romaine, butter lettuce, green- and red-leaf lettuces are all excellent choices. These are no-brainers for no-waste gardening because they practically grow themselves. You can keep several heads going in the same bowl or container at once, too. For rerooting, buy romaine heads or hydroponic lettuce that still has the base of the plant stem or roots attached.

When you attempt to reroot head lettuces, they may or may not grow new roots, but in any case the heads will usually give you eight to ten more leaves per plant, depending on the type. Any new leaves will not be as large as the original leaves, but they're enough to put on sandwiches or bulk up your salads. Sometimes the inner core of the bottom of the plant will rot. If that happens, just throw it out or add it to your compost.

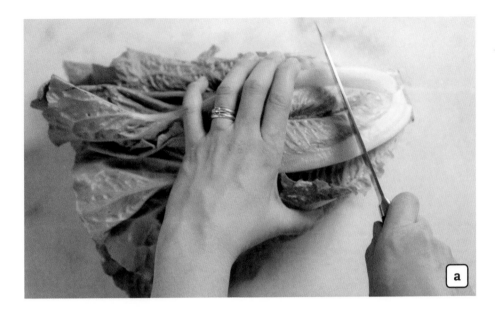

How to Regrow Lettuce

You will need a cup or bowl; a clean, sharp knife; and toothpicks (optional).

1. Fill the glass or bowl with about an inch of water.

2. Make a fresh cut at the top of the head of lettuce, leaving about 3 inches of lettuce. This ensures that you don't cut off the growing tip, which needs to be on the plant if you want it to continue to grow new leaves. [a]

3. **Optional step:** If you want to suspend the lettuce in the glass rather than having the bottom of the lettuce rest on the bottom, stick three or four toothpicks evenly spaced around the lettuce, about 1 inch up from the bottom. The toothpicks will suspend the lettuce from the sides of the glass.

4. Place the lettuce in the water. Make sure that no more than 1 inch of the bottom of the plant is covered, whether you are placing the plant directly in the cup or suspending it with toothpicks. [b]

5. Set the cup or bowl in an area of bright, indirect light. The more light, the longer you'll get lettuce, the bigger the leaves will grow, and the greener and more flavorful they'll be.

6. Change the water every couple of days.

Harvest and Keep Growing!

Snip off new leaves as they grow for use in salads or sandwiches, until the plant starts bolting.

As a fun experiment, plant the rooted lettuce plant outside and allow it to flower so that you can save seeds. What you get when you plant your saved seeds depends on whether the original plant was open pollinated or is an F-1 hybrid, but it will be fun to follow the plants through their entire growing cycle, and you'll get something you can eat—perhaps something a little unexpected.

fun fact

Lettuce originated in the Mediterranean region, and varieties with long, thick stems and pointy leaves are depicted in ancient Egyptian tomb paintings. The romaine lettuce that we eat today is likely closely related to these ancient lettuces. The first crisphead type of lettuce, or what we refer to as "iceberg lettuce," was developed and introduced in 1941. 'Great Lakes,' the first crisphead variety, is still grown today.

growing tip

Lettuce is a "long day" plant. It will start flowering when it receives 12 or more hours of light per day, which happens during the summer. At that point you can gather the seeds. Heat can also cause bolting in lettuce, because it's a cool-weather green. If you plant regrown lettuces outside, your best chance to get seeds is in the late spring and early summer.

Buy celery by the bunch with the bottom intact if you want to regrow it.

CELERY

Celery is another no-brainer for regrowing. Celery bunches that you purchase still have a lot of life left in them, as long as they are intact. They will easily regrow from a growing tip tucked among the stalks. You can't reroot celery stalks that are not attached to the rest of the celery bunch: celery stalks are actually leaf stalks (or *petioles*) that don't have any growing buds on them.

Celery is the foundation of many soups, casseroles, and salads. You can't beat it for low-calorie crunch. When you regrow celery, you'll notice that the flavor of the new stalks is much more intense than what you originally purchased.

How to Regrow Celery

You will need a cup or bowl and a sharp knife.

1. Fill a glass or bowl with about an inch of water.

2. Prepare the celery by cutting off the top cleanly about 3 inches above the bottom of the bunch. The center is where the plant will regrow. (a)

3. Place the plant in the water. Make sure that no more than 1 inch of the bottom of the plant is covered. (b)

4. Set the cup or bowl in an area of bright, indirect light. The more light, the longer your regrowing celery will last and the greener the new stalks will be.

5. Change the water every few days. With celery, this is an especially necessary step as the water will grow cloudy and smelly if you leave it alone.

6. Tear off any stalk remnants that are rotting to keep the plant tidy while you enjoy the new stalks.

growing tip

Celery is a cool-weather plant. If you want to try regrowing it outside, plant during the spring or the fall. You'll get the biggest second crop by planting in late summer and harvesting in late fall before a frost.

Harvest and Keep Growing!

Once you start seeing roots emerge, you can transplant the celery plant into soil. Bury the rooted plant so that just about ½ inch is sticking out of the soil. When you see new stalks emerging, cover up the remains of the old stalks with a little bit of soil. (This will keep the pot from attracting fruit flies and will simply tidy it up.)

Celery is a heavy drinker, so keep the soil consistently moist but not sopping wet. Break off stalks as you need them, always leaving a few on the plant to keep producing food for the plant. At some point a flower stalk will emerge from the center of the plant. Let it grow and flower, and you can save the resulting celery seed for use in cooking. You can also try to grow your own celery from seed.

After the celery bunch grows roots, plant it in a pot or outside to keep growing.

GREEN (BUNCHING) ONIONS

Green onions (also known as *bunching onions* or *scallions*) add zest to any savory recipe. But they can be expensive and tend to wilt and get slimy quickly, so it makes more sense to grow some on your kitchen counter to have a steady fresh supply on hand.

Green onions are almost always sold in bunches, and each individual onion is an entire plant. The roots are at the bottom, followed by a white-colored compressed stem and leaves. You can regrow bunching onions in water as easily as in soil. After rerooting in water, you can also transplant them into soil for a longer-lasting harvest—or you can grow them directly in soil. To learn how to do that, mimic the directions for growing leeks in soil on page 68. But here's how to grow them in water, which will likely result in less mess than the soil method.

These green onions have been regrown in soil and are ready to eat!

How to Regrow Green Onions

You will need a cup or bowl, a sharp knife, and some pebbles.

1. Prepare the onions for rooting by cutting off the green tops and leaving about an inch of the stem (mostly white) attached to the roots at the very bottom. (a)

2. Fill the bottom of the cup or bowl with ½ to ¾ inch of clean pebbles.

3. Fill a cup or bowl with water so that the pebbles are covered with ½ inch of water.

4. Place the bottoms of the onions in the pebbles, making sure that the pieces are half submerged. **b**

5. Set the cup or bowl in an area of bright, indirect light. The more light, the longer your regrowing onions will last.

6. Change the water every couple of days.

Harvest and Keep Growing!

Snip off the young green leaves for use on top of soups, to add flavor to sandwiches, and for stirring into salads.

Keep your green onion harvest growing longer by planting the rooted cuttings in potting soil or into the garden outside. Green onions grow best during cool weather, so plant them outside during the spring or fall.

fun fact

During the American Civil War, in 1864, United States General Ulysses S. Grant famously said, "I will not move my army without onions!" Getting food to the troops was difficult, and onions were used for medicinal as well as culinary purposes.

FENNEL

Fennel has a licorice-like taste and is a frequent ingredient in Mediterranean recipes. The whole plant is edible, including the flowers and the seeds, which you probably have in your spice rack. When cooking with fresh fennel, it's the ferny leaf tops or the crunchy bottoms of the leaves (the white bulb) that you're after.

Fennel grows in a manner similar to celery. Both have a growing tip surrounded by modified leaves, which are

This photo shows a fennel bulb cut in half. You can really see the growing tip inside of the bulb, which, as you know, is a modified stem.

the parts that we most commonly eat. In order to regrow fennel, buy bulbs with the bottoms intact.

If you aren't currently cooking with fennel, you might want to dream up a reason to do so—these are very pretty houseplants while they are regrowing.

How to Regrow Fennel

You will need a cup or bowl, sharp knife, alcohol, and toothpicks (optional).

1. Cut off the top of the fennel plant, leaving about 2 inches of the bulb intact.

2. Fill a cup or bowl with water to use for rerooting. You want the bottom half of the bulb to be covered when it is sitting in the cup, so if using toothpicks to suspend the bulb in the glass, fill up the entire glass. If you're going to put the bulb in the bowl or cup, fill the container with about 1 inch of water.

3. Place the plant in the water. (If suspending via toothpicks, stick the toothpicks into the bulb about halfway between the bottom and top.) Make sure that no more than 1 inch of the bottom of the plant is covered with water. ⓑ

4. Set the container in an area of bright, indirect light. The more light, the longer your cutting will last and the more leaves you'll get.

5. Change the water every couple of days.

After the celery bunch grows roots, plant it in a pot or outside to keep growing.

Harvest and Keep Growing!

If you prefer to use mostly the leafy fronds and not the tougher bottom parts of the leaves or bulb, you can just cut off the fronds for cooking, leaving the whole bulb intact to keep growing.

When the plant has grown new roots or is starting to sprout shoots, you can plant it in soil. Leave about ½ inch of the leftover plant sticking up until you have three or four new stalks, and then cover it completely with soil.

Fennel will eventually flower and produce seed, which is great for use in cooking. It will cross-pollinate with other plants in the same family (such as carrots or dill) if they bloom at the same time, so new seeds might or might not germinate if you replant them—better to instead use them in cooking.

It's easy and fun to root herb stem cuttings in water.

HERB STEM CUTTINGS

Herbs are your best bet for rooting cuttings in water. A cutting is simply a piece of plant. Stem cuttings include a 3- to 4-inch piece of stem with the growing tip still intact at the top, a few sets of leaves, and a few inches of stem at the bottom of the cutting. Look for supple, non-flowering stems of these plants. If you're taking cuttings from your garden, spring and early summer are ideal, as there will be lots of fresh, young growth. If you plan to perpetuate your purchases, while grocery shopping look for herbs with clean stems. You don't want to cook with slimy herbs, and you won't have good results regrowing them either.

The process for regrowing most herbs is the same. Here are some that are easy to regrow:

- Basil
- Cilantro
- Lemon balm
- Mint
- Oregano
- Parsley
- Sage
- Thyme

How to Regrow
Herb Stem Cuttings

You will need a clear glass jar (so you can watch the roots grow!), clean water, a clean towel, snips or kitchen scissors, and Lysol® or isopropyl alcohol.

growing tip

Keep basil growing strong all summer by continuously rooting a fresh supply of transplants. When plants have been in the ground a few weeks, snip the tip, bring inside, and root.

a

1. Wash the glass jar that you'll use for rooting. Use a clean towel to dry the jar. (You don't want to introduce any bacteria or fungi that could cause the cuttings to rot.)

2. Fill the jar with room temperature water. If you have heavily chlorinated water, you might want to let it sit (covered) for few days before using it.

3. Disinfect the snips or scissors with Lysol® or isopropyl alcohol.

4. Prepare the cuttings by removing any of the leaves from the bottom 2 to 3 inches of the plant, because they would be underwater in the glass jar. Just pinch off the leaves close to the stem. a

b

5. Hold the cuttings under a running tap and snip off the bottoms so they have a fresh cut.

6. Immediately place the cuttings in water. ⓑ

7. Set the jar in an area of bright light but not in direct afternoon sunlight.

8. Change the water every few days to keep it fresh and free of bacteria and fungal diseases.

Harvest and Keep Growing!

All stem cuttings from herb plants root fairly easily. Different plants take different amounts of time to root. Some will grow roots in as few as 4 or 5 days, and some might take up to 2 weeks. The softer cuttings do tend to root faster than woodier cuttings, such as those from rosemary or sage.

Herbs fall into two of the categories discussed in Chapter 1. Some of them are annuals or biennials (cilantro, basil, parsley) and others are perennials (mint, sage, rosemary). It's good to know which type you're growing, because then you'll know what to expect.

If you want the herbs to grow enough to produce more leaves to harvest, you'll want to pot them up to enjoy indoors or out. You can start harvesting a few leaves at a time once the plants start producing new leaves.

Eventually, annual herbs will flower and set seed. At that point, they're basically done and destined for the compost heap. Perennial herbs will keep growing. They may go dormant during the winter, but will leaf out again in the spring.

All herbs grow well outdoors in full sun.

Basil will regrow easily indoors in bright sunlight.

growing tip

Herbs need quite a bit of light, so if you plan to grow them indoors in pots, investigate a small grow-light setup. Otherwise, once they've settled into their new containers, move them to a bright, sunny windowsill and enjoy them for as long as they produce. Then root more! If you've potted up new plants during the summer, let them grow a bit in the pots, then transplant outside into the garden. It's always a good idea to harden off transplants before putting them in the garden. For a few days, set the pots in a partially shaded area that is protected from winds. Then plant plants in the garden.

When you buy a pineapple, you get a two-for-one deal: a fruit and a new plant on top of the fruit.

PINEAPPLE

Regrowing a pineapple is considered something of a holy grail of regrowing edibles—a sign that you are truly serious about the craft. It can take a few attempts to see results, so try not to get discouraged if the first go-around doesn't take.

Regrowing pineapples is really a matter of rerooting the entire plant. Pineapples are members of the bromeliad family, many of which reproduce by growing new plants (pups) when the center plant flowers. The top of a pineapple is such a pup. It will eventually flower and produce the fruit we know as a pineapple. (This can take several years.)

This exercise follows a formula of "higher input = higher reward." It is a source of considerable pride when you can point to a pineapple plant with a little pineapple forming on it and say, "I grew that." It's not something everyone succeeds at.

How to Regrow a Pineapple

You will need a sharp knife, a cup, toothpicks, potting soil, a flowerpot with an 8- to 12-inch diameter, and a watering can.

1. To prepare the pineapple top for rooting, firmly grasp with one hand the top by the base, close to where it attaches to the pineapple, and hold the pineapple fruit in the other hand. (a)

2. Twist and pull up on the top until you've removed it from the fruit.

3. Strip off the bottom one-third of the leaves, exposing the stem. (b)

4. Use a sharp knife to cut off the bottom ½ inch of the stem, then remove any fruit that is still attached to the bottom of the stem.

5. Place the pineapple stem in a cup of water. If you wish, you can use toothpicks to suspend the pineapple top in the cup so just the bottom rests in the water. (c)

6. Allow the stem to grow roots and new leaves. Once it has grown both, it is ready to be transplanted into a pot. Tend it carefully, and be prepared for a long period of nurturing before an edible fruit is ready.

Keep Growing!

When you see roots developing on the pineapple stem, transplant it into a flowerpot. Bury the rooted area and the bottom of the stem about 2 inches deep. You can trim off any drying leaves or parts of leaves at this point.

The pineapple will eventually start to grow new leaves from the center of the plant. It can take up to 9 months for the plant to go from a top piece rooting in water to growing in soil. It can be 2 or more years before the plant produces fruit, but it's fun to grow in the meantime. Keep the pineapple in bright light indoors. If you want to move it outdoors during the summer, harden it off by placing it in a protected, somewhat shady spot for a few days before moving it out into the sun.

If you regrow pineapples, you'll always have a conversation piece.

Resources

This book is meant to be used as a reference to help you get started growing things you have on hand. To go to the next level and grow a larger garden outdoors, you'll want some more references. Here are some of my favorite books for growing an outdoor garden.

Beginner's Illustrated Guide to Gardening: Techniques to Help You Get Started, by Katie Elzer-Peters. Cool Springs Press, 2012.

Container Gardening Complete: Creative Projects for Growing Vegetables and Flowers in Small Spaces, by Jessica Walliser. Cool Springs Press, 2017.

DIY Projects for the Self-Sufficient Homeowner: 25 Ways to Build a Self-Reliant Lifestyle, by Betsy Matheson. Cool Springs Press, 2011.

Foodscaping: Practical and Innovative Ways to Create an Edible Landscape, by Charlie Nardozzi. Cool Springs Press, 2015.

The Home Orchard Handbook: A Complete Guide to Growing Your Own Fruit Trees Anywhere, by Cem Akin and Leah Rottke. Cool Springs Press, 2011.

Perennial Vegetables: From Artichoke to Zuiki Taro, a Gardener's Guide to Over 100 Delicious, Easy-to-grow Edibles, by Eric Toensmeier. Chelsea Green Publications, 2007.

Practical Organic Gardening: The No-Nonsense Guide to Growing Naturally, by Mark Highland. Cool Springs Press, 2017.

Pruning, An Illustrated Guide: Foolproof Methods for Shaping and Trimming Trees, Shrubs, Vines, and More, by Judy Lowe. Cool Springs Press, 2014.

Raised Bed Revolution: Build It, Fill It, Plant It ... Garden Anywhere!, by Tara Nolen. Cool Springs Press, 2016.

Index

ACKNOWLEDGMENTS

I write books because I love writing books, and I'm so grateful to you, the reader, for picking this book up and, hopefully, having fun with it. Without readers, we don't need writers.

Many people have helped shepherd this book from an idea to a beautiful reality. Kirsten Boehmer, my photographer, has taken gorgeous photos of what can be, quite frankly, some ugly-looking kitchen scraps. I wouldn't have wanted to embark on this project with anyone else. Every writer needs editors, and I appreciate Alyssa Lochner and the copyeditors and horticultural editors who whipped my writing into shape. It's all just words until the art directors get their hands on everything and shape it into something you'd like to read and study, so we can all be thankful for them. I camped out many afternoons at Spoonfed Kitchen & Bakeshop in Wilmington, North Carolina, to write. They kept my tea glass full, played my favorite boy-band music, and let me raid their compost bin for kitchen scraps to regrow. (Kim and Matt, those are your beets!) As with all my work, I could never complete a book without the patience, dish-washing, and meal-fetching of my darling husband or without the support and love of my parents, Bob and Joy.

PHOTO CREDITS

Photography by Kirsten Boehmer, except the following:

Shutterstock, pages: 10 top, photosync; 10 bottom, Kazakova Maryia; 11, Rimma Bondarenko; 12, akiyoko; 13, Graham Corney; 15, zhekoss; 16 left, Vanitytheone; 16 right, sichkarenko.com; 17, lauraslens; 19, asadykov; 20 top, Africa Studio; 20 bottom, Bosnian; 27, Gary Perkin; 32, Kymme; 36, Lotus Images; 38, Swapan Photography; 39, PosiNote; 54, tamu1500; 55, marekuliasz; 59, JeepFoto; 61, tag2016; 62, Ishchuk Olena; 64, Rostovtsevayu; 65 bottom, polaris50d; page 72, Olya Detry; page 74, Mariusz S. Jurgielewicz; page 79, Garsya; 80, locrifa; 83, Cora Mueller; 85, Ivan Masiuk; 87, Swellphotography; 88, DenisNata; 89, Donald Joski; 90, Dean Stuart Jarvis; 91, tchara; 92, Anna Grigorjeva; 93, NataliaL; 94, Ilzira; 95, Catalin Petolea; 97 top left, Aleksandar Grozdanovski; 97 top right, fotocat5; 100 left, Subbotina Anna; 113 bottom, Viktor1; 119, Fausta Lavagna; 120, Dmitrij Skorobogatov; 122, Norrabhudi; 123, Viktoriia Drobotova.

Illustrations by Shutterstock/Ann Doronina and Shutterstock/mart

ABOUT THE AUTHOR

KATIE ELZER-PETERS has been gardening since she could walk. She earned a Bachelor of Science in Public Horticulture from Purdue University and a Master of Science in Public Garden Management from the Longwood Graduate Program at Longwood Gardens and the University of Delaware.

After completing her studies, Katie served as a horticulturist, head of gardens, educational programs director, development officer, and manager of botanical gardens around the United States. Katie has authored eight other books for Cool Springs Press, including *Beginner's Illustrated Guide to Gardening: Techniques to Help You Get Started*; *Miniature Gardens: Design and create miniature fairy gardens, dish gardens, terrariums and more—indoors and out*; *Mid-Atlantic Gardener's Handbook*, and five books about vegetable gardening. She has ghostwritten and edited dozens of other gardening books and serves as the editor-in-chief of *The Designer*, the quarterly journal of the Association of Professional Landscape Designers.

Today, Katie lives and gardens with her husband and dogs in the coastal city of Wilmington, North Carolina, (zone 8) where she owns The Garden of Words, LLC, a marketing and PR firm specializing in garden-industry clients.